240 Family Devotions Based on the Words of Jesus

NOT-
So-Quiet Times

Tracy Harrast

Standard
Publishing
Cincinnati, Ohio

Standard Publishing, a division of Standex International Corporation, Cincinnati, Ohio.
© 2000 by Tracy L. Harrast. All rights reserved.
Bean Sprouts™ and the Bean Sprouts design logo are
trademarks of Standard Publishing.

Printed in the United States of America.
ISBN 0-7847-1041-4

Project editor: Lise Caldwell. Design: Liz Howe Design.
Typesetting by Andrew Quach. Author photo by Deborah Safaie.

07 06 05 04 03 02 01 00   5 4 3 2 1

Library of Congress Cataloging-in-Publication Data

Harrast, Tracy L.
Not-so-quiet times: 240 family devotions based on the words of Jesus / by Tracy L. Harrast.
p. cm.
ISBN 0-7847-1041-4
1. Children–Prayer-books and devotions–English. 2. Family–Prayer-books and devotions–English.
I. Title.

BV4571.2.H375 2000
249–dc21   99-055975

Dedication

For Sharon Tebbe,
Her love for God shows in the way she loves everyone around her.

Acknowledgments

Robin Harrast, my husband: I've loved you since the moment you tied my ice skate twenty years ago. Amy Harrast: It makes me happy to watch how you grow the many gifts God has given you. Your beautiful songs bring tears to my eyes. Lauren Harrast: You're a ray of light in my life. Your compassion for everyone warms my heart, and your jokes crack me up. Ryan Harrast: You have a pure heart. I'm very thankful for such a lovable son who cares so much for others. All day long I look forward to your after-school hug. Harry Leffingwell, my dad: Thanks for the good launch you and Mom gave me. We've all been blessed by having you move in with our family. Cheryl Dickson, my sister: I miss you and your chocolate chip cookies. Chris Bullion, my cousin: Thanks for caring and for making me laugh out loud when I read your e-mails. Ever since we were little, I've wished you were my brother. My Harrast in-laws, nephews, and nieces: Leon, Eleanor, Chris, Steve, Michelle, Carol, John, Sonja, Tim, Mariana, Ken, Susan, Kine, Britte, Stephanie, Denise, Terrell, Heather, Mary Ruth, Andrew, Bradley, Porter, Emily, Amanda, and Daniel: I love each of you and feel privileged to be in the same family with you. Lise Caldwell and Diane Stortz, at Standard Publishing: Thanks for helping this book become its best. You have the gift of encouragement. Lynne Davis, Glenda McCloskey, and Gay Smith: You are the kindest and most loving friends anyone could ever hope to have. God uses you as visual aids to show me how to live what his Word says. Kim Myer, my sweet friend since we were ten: Thanks for commiserating during all the hard times and cheerleading during all the good times. Jane Ferguson: Thanks for taking my kids to the pool while I wrote. You make it easy to "love my neighbor."

WHAT'S INSIDE
This Book

More Good Stuff

GETTING STARTED
and Sticking With It!

A Few Pointers

◎ **Find the time of day that works best for your family devotions.**
First thing in the morning? Before breakfast? With after-school snacks? During dinner? Before your kids' favorite show? After baths? Before bedtime?

◎ **If you miss your regular time, grab a minute when you can.**
Skim the devotion yourself and then talk about it on the go. You can even discuss the day's verse with the kids while you're reaching for the baby shampoo or waiting for a red light to change—but don't drop the book in the tub or out the car window!

Find the Time

◎ **Involve the whole family!** If both parents can be involved in the devotions and take turns teaching them, the kids understand that God's Word is important to both their mom and their dad. Besides, devotions are more fun if the whole family is involved!

Stay Flexible!

✹ **Don't hesitate to customize the devotions** for your family. If your youngest kids can't write, let them draw or dictate to you while the others write. If any memory verses are too long for the youngest kids, select a shorter section of the verse for them to memorize. Feel free to use other translations of the Bible if you wish.

✹ **Don't be discouraged** if the kids are rambunctious at first while testing their boundaries. Keep things casual (translate: no assigned seats in the family room) so the kids don't tune you out

because things are too stiff. The less the devotion feels like school, the more they'll like it. Remember, "Do not exasperate your children; instead, bring them up in the training and instruction of the Lord" (Ephesians 6:4).

* **Relax and enjoy yourself.** The goal is for everyone (even you!) to have fun while learning. Get down and romp with those kids! They will remember playing with you and learning together for the rest of their lives.

* **Each day before you skim the devotion,** ask the Lord to give the kids listening ears and to plant his Word deep into everyone's heart. Then let the Holy Spirit lead the way. If he gives you a different way to teach the devotion, go for it!

* **When you're tempted to skip devotion time,** repeat to yourself over and over: "It's important! It's quick! It's easy!"

* **Usually if you just give the devotions a quick skim,** you're good to go. If you can, glance at a week's worth at a time. (Sunday afternoon might be a good time.) If the Attention Grabbers use any materials at all, the items will usually be things you already have on hand, but glance at the supply list on pages 257-260 to be sure you will have everything you need. On days when you don't have time or materials, just skip the attention grabber and go on to the Living It section.

Keep With It

... **Even if** you only have time to read the day's verse.

... **Even if** you're on vacation.

... **Even if** somebody has the chicken pox.

... **Even if** you've missed a day or a week.

Don't let anything stop you from doing devotions.

Fix these words of mine in your hearts and minds. ... Teach them to your children, talking about them when you sit at home and when you walk along the road, when you lie down and when you get up.
Deuteronomy 11:18, 19

HOW TO LEAD
These Devotions

Memory Verse

You will be amazed at how much faster kids memorize than adults. Hide God's Word in their hearts and they'll use the verses throughout their lives.

◎ Provide a Know-It-By-Heart Chart for each family member (page 261). Photocopy the chart if you need more than two.

◎ Try to memorize a verse each day or as often as possible.

◎ See tips for memorization on pages 14–15.

Attention Grabber

The fun you'll have during these activities will unite your family, help the kids focus, and make the devotions memorable.

◎ Whenever an activity requires extra time or slightly unusual materials, you will find a simple option, too. If you have the time and materials, do the longer version. If time or supplies are limited, do the faster version.

◎ If you're in a pinch, don't worry if you need to skip over this section and get right to Living It. Never let lack of time for this section keep you from doing the devotion.

◎ If you can, skim these briefly in advance. Check the supplies list on pages 257–260 weekly or monthly to be sure you have everything you'll need. You will probably already have most of the items on hand. Some activities require only imagination!

◎ In most cases, pique their curiosity with the Attention Grabber before reading the Memory Verse. But if your time is too limited, let the older kids do the Attention Grabbers as fun follow-ups.

Living It

This is when you make the point. Explain the verse and show the kids how to apply it to their lives.

- You may wish to begin this section by reading the entire Bible passage cited at the top of the devotion, or by telling the Bible story.
- This section is written so you can read it directly out of the book; however, it will be even more interesting to the kids if you say it in your own words.
- Add examples from family members' lives whenever possible.

Discussion Questions

This section gets the kids flexing their brain muscles.

- Some of the questions are rhetorical. Let the kids know which they need to just think about and which they should answer aloud.
- Pay attention to the kids' responses to see what kind of follow-up, one-on-one discussion they may need.
- Some questions are geared toward older kids. It's OK to skip these with younger children.

Prayer Prompter

Always end the devotion with prayer so the kids will learn to rely on God. Praying together will draw your family close.

- Let the Prayer Prompter focus your family's attention on the spiritual lesson God is impressing on your hearts.
- Each day ask everyone in the family to share at least one prayer request or praise for his or her own life or the lives of friends and family. In addition to praying for God's help to apply the devotion, pray for everyone's personal needs.

TIPS
for Memorizing Bible Verses

◉ When memorizing verses, memorize the references, too.

◉ Recite the day's verse several times while preparing and eating breakfast. Ask each child to repeat it at least once before leaving for school or beginning homeschool studies.

◉ Write the verse on the bathroom mirror with a dry-erase marker stored in the bathroom drawer.

◉ If there's enough time, you or the kids can write the verse on their lunch sacks or paper napkins.

◉ Buy small dot stickers in a different color for each family member. Whoever remembers the day's verse at dinnertime gets to stick his or her color of dot on a Know-It-By-Heart Chart (page 261).

◉ At dinnertime, ask who thought of the verse during the day. How did it help?

◉ Offer special incentives to be awarded on Fridays (for example, a video rental or trip to the park) if everyone in the family can remember all five of the week's memory verses.

◉ Music makes verses easier to memorize. Consider buying cassettes that teach Bible verses through songs. Or simply make up your own songs by singing each verse to a familiar tune (such as "Mary Had a Little Lamb").

◉ Use the day's verse as a password that everyone must recite to enter the house or one another's bedrooms.

- Tape verses to the TV remote control and computer monitor.

- Seal the verses between sticky sides of two pieces of Con-Tact self-adhesive cover. Cut into shapes. Wet these "water stickers," and they'll stick to the bathtub or shower wall for memorizing while you scrub-a-dub-dub.

- Tape copies of verses to food or treats the kids can have once they memorize the verse. Try wrapping a verse around the shell of a hard-boiled egg or a stick of gum.

- Tape the verses to the back of the cereal box so kids will stare at them while they eat.

- Have the kids tape the day's verse around their pencils so they can read it during breaks at school.

- Let the kids write verses on the sidewalk with colored chalk.

- Set monthly goals for the family together. Have everyone help those who are struggling until they meet the goal so you can have a family Memorization Celebration.

Not on Bread Alone
Matthew 4:1-4

Memory Verse

Jesus answered, "It is written: 'Man does not live on bread alone, but on every word that comes from the mouth of God'" (Matthew 4:4).

Attention Grabber

Cut the crusts off slices of bread. Let each child fold a slice vertically so it is shaped like a Bible. Explain that bread and the Bible are both food. One is food for our bodies and the other is food for our spirits. If you have time, make the bread into cinnamon toast.

Living It

Our spirits may not demand food the way our bodies do, but both need food to stay strong. Our spirits are fed when we talk to God and listen to him in our prayers and read his written Word, the Bible. Part of this verse comes from the Old Testament. Jesus memorized that verse and quoted it when the devil tried to tempt him. Knowing God's Word helps us fight temptations, too.

Discussion Questions

- If we were out of bread for a week, would you notice?
- If your Bible were in the Lost and Found for a week, would you miss it?
- Do you feel and treat others better when your spirit has been fed? Why or why not?

Prayer Prompter

Help us spend time with you daily so our spirits are fed. Help us memorize Bible verses and remember them when we're tempted.

Don't Test God
Matthew 4:5-7

Memory Verse
Jesus answered him, "It is also written: 'Do not put the Lord your God to the test'" (Matthew 4:7).

Attention Grabber
Ask the kids what others have dared them to do. How did they like being dared? Have they ever taken a dare? Talk about typical dares and their consequences. Emphasize that dares are usually against our better judgment.

Living It
God doesn't like to be tested or dared either! He has the power to do anything, but he doesn't want people to try to force him to prove it. He wants us to ask for his help when we genuinely need it, having faith that he has the power to help us. It would be wrong to put ourselves in a dangerous situation just to test whether God would help us. The devil tried to get Jesus to jump off a tall building to prove that angels would catch him. Jesus wouldn't do it. If we break physical laws to test whether God will do a miracle, he might let us suffer the physical consequences. It's wrong to test or dare God this way, whether it's physically dangerous or not.

Discussion Questions
⊙ In what situations would it be right to ask God for a miracle?
⊙ What are some miracles God has done for our family, someone we know, or someone we have read about?

Prayer Prompter
Please give us the faith to ask for miracles when we sincerely need them, but prevent us from making disrespectful requests for the wrong reasons.

Worship God Only

Memory Verse
Jesus said to him, "Away from me, Satan! For it is written: 'Worship the Lord your God, and serve him only'" (Matthew 4:10).

Attention Grabber
Have the kids imagine that the fanciest chair you own is God's throne. Have them set flimsier chairs beside it. Explain that sometimes we fall for Satan's tricks and give most of our time, attention, and trust to other things, such as money, belongings, or popularity. Have the kids remove the chairs. Emphasize that we need to stop worshiping anything except God.

Living It
Sometimes the devil directly asks people to worship him. There are people who practice witchcraft and listen to Satanic music. However, the devil is sneakier than that with most of us. He tempts us to fill our need for God with other things. Anything that takes too much of our time, attention, and trust away from God can become like a god in our life. We need to be sure we worship only the true God.

Discussion Questions
- Has anything become a false god in your life by getting too much of your time, attention, and trust?
- How can you focus on God more in your daily life? (Look up Colossians 3:23 and Matthew 25:40.)

Prayer Prompter
Please help us worship you and serve you throughout our everyday life. Please keep us from relying on anything else as a god instead of you.

Repent!
Matthew 4:17; Mark 1:15

Memory Verse
From that time on Jesus began to preach, "Repent, for the kingdom of heaven is near" (Matthew 4:17).

Attention Grabber
Act like a drill sergeant (or let kids take turns having that role) and tell the "troops" to march around your home. Occasionally tell them "about-face!"

Living It
What is an "about-face"? (Turning away from one direction to another.) Repenting is like doing an "about-face." It means to turn away from sin toward God. Repentance was so important to Jesus that it was the first thing he talked about to the people in Galilee. He wanted them—and us—to turn away from sin and look to him instead. As soon as we see that we are heading into sin, let's do an "about-face" from it quickly and ask God to forgive us.

Discussion Questions
◎ What would happen if you didn't do an "about-face" when you marched toward obstacles in our home? (You would reach a dead end, trip over them, possibly get hurt.)
◎ How is that like not repenting from sin?

Prayer Prompter
Please forgive us for the wrong things we have done. Give us the strength to turn away from our sins.

Be Fishers of People
Matthew 4:18-21

Memory Verse

"Come, follow me," Jesus said, *"and I will make you fishers of men"* *(Matthew 4:19).*

Attention Grabber

Ask the kids if they've seen the "Jesus Fish" (ichthus) on bumper stickers or t-shirts. Have them draw it. If they draw this symbol on white Con-Tact self-adhesive cover, they can make stickers for their bikes. Explain that the fish is a symbol for Christians. You can tell older children that it is because the letters of the Greek word for "fish" (ichthus) are the first letters for the Greek words that mean Jesus Christ, God's Son, Savior.

Living It

Matthew 13:47-50 says the kingdom of heaven is like a net. People are like fish that God wants to come into the net. If we follow Jesus, he uses us to show people the truth. The truth about Jesus draws them into his kingdom as fish are drawn into a net.

Discussion Questions

◉ When have you been a "fisher of men" and told about Jesus?
◉ Are you glad someone told you about Jesus?
◉ How will other people feel if we tell them about him?

Prayer Prompter

Show us when and how to share the truth about you so people will believe and come into your kingdom.

The Poor in Spirit
Matthew 5:1-3

Memory Verse
"Blessed are the poor in spirit, for theirs is the kingdom of heaven"
(Matthew 5:3).

Attention Grabber
Ask the kids to act out or simply recite a football cheer or two. Emphasize that sometimes we feel "full of spirit" and sometimes we don't.

Living It
Jesus' sayings that begin "Blessed are the ..." are called "beatitudes." In his first beatitude, Jesus told his followers that we have reason to be happy even when we're "poor in spirit." God has blessed us with a great inheritance: heaven is ours! It can be a great encouragement to focus on heaven when we're discouraged. Also, when we humbly realize how much we need God, we can reach out to him more. When you hang your head in discouragement, turn to him and he will "lift your head" (Psalm 3:3).

Discussion Questions
◉ In what situations has God "lifted your head" when you were "poor in spirit"?
◉ How can focusing on heaven encourage us?

Prayer Prompters
When we are discouraged, help us open up to you and let you encourage us. Help us remember what you have in store for us in heaven.

The Holy Spirit Comforts
Matthew 5:4

Memory Verse
"Blessed are those who mourn, for they will be comforted"
(Matthew 5:4).

Attention Grabber
See if a comforter from a bed can wrap around your entire family if you hug tightly enough. Ask the kids why they think this bed-cover is called a "comforter."

Living It
Jesus told his followers that we have reason to be happy even when we mourn. To mourn means to be terribly sad, usually about the death of a loved one. It can also mean other sadness, such as when we have sinned. If we turn to God when we mourn, God will comfort us. One of the names of his Holy Spirit is "the Comforter," because he consoles us and eases our sadness. Revelation 21:4 promises that in heaven God will "wipe every tear from their eyes. There will be no more death or mourning or crying or pain, for the old order of things has passed away."

Discussion Questions
- How are a bed's comforter and the Holy Spirit similar?
- If we are sad about our sins, how can we get God's comfort? (Ask him to forgive us because Jesus took the punishment for us. Tell him we are sorry.)

Prayer Prompters
Please comfort us when we are very sad. Help us remember that we won't have any sadness in heaven.

Meek, Not Weak
Matthew 5:5

Memory Verse
"Blessed are the meek, for they will inherit the earth"
(Matthew 5:5).

Attention Grabber
Pin a towel like a cape to the youngest child's clothes and let the child pretend to be a superhero. Mention that if someone teased a superhero about his tights or the gel in his hair, that superhero would have the physical strength to fight back. The kind of strength we need is strength of character to *resist* fighting back.

Living It
To be meek before God means to be humble, realizing his greatness and power over us and how much we need him. Meekness toward other people means to be gentle with them. It means being brave enough not to fight back or put yourself above them. Philippians 2:3, 4 says, "Do nothing out of selfish ambition or vain conceit, but in humility consider others better than yourselves. Each of you should look not only to your own interests, but also to the interests of others." Sometimes people who are selfish and pushy seem to "get ahead," but in the end, the whole earth will belong to Jesus' meek followers.

Discussion Questions
◉ How is meek different from weak? (If you're weak, you treat others better because you have to. If you're meek, you treat others better because you want to, which takes strength.)
◉ Is it easy to be meek? Why or why not?

Prayer Prompter
Please help us to be meek and humble before you and gentle with other people.

Meek, Not Weak

Hungry and Thirsty

Memory Verse
"Blessed are those who hunger and thirst for righteousness, for they will be filled" (Matthew 5:6).

Attention Grabber
Offer the kids a salty snack without a drink. Then ask them to describe the time they have been most thirsty. Have one of them dramatize what it would be like to walk through the desert with an empty canteen. Have the child show how he or she would act when approaching an oasis. Then offer everyone a cold drink.

Living It
To be righteous means to be "right with God." None of us feels peaceful until we are right with God. It is like being very hungry or thirsty—you aren't satisfied until you have what you need. All of us need God to forgive our sins so we can be right with him. Romans 10:4 says, "Christ is the end of the law so that there may be righteousness for everyone who believes." People who believe Jesus died to take away their sins, and who ask God to forgive them, become right with God and find peace.

Discussion Questions
- Do you ever feel "hungry" to be right with God?
- Have you asked Jesus to be your Savior so that you are right with God? (Turn to page 268 for help in discussing this with your child.)

Prayer Prompter
Please forgive us for what we have done wrong, because Jesus died for us. Please make us right with you.

Have Mercy!
Matthew 5:7

Memory Verse
"Blessed are the merciful, for they will be shown mercy"
(Matthew 5:7).

Attention Grabber
Tickle the children until they beg you to stop. Say, "I showed you mercy." Ask, "If you were the 'tickler' instead of the 'tickle-ee' would you want to stop when I asked you?" Explain that we want mercy for ourselves; but when we have power, it's tempting not to give mercy to others.

Living It
When we need help, kindness, or forgiveness, we want others to have mercy on us. Yet sometimes we're not as eager to offer that mercy to others. We might feel we don't have to be merciful if the other person doesn't deserve it. God is so merciful that he helps and forgives us even though we don't deserve it. Titus 3:5 says that God "saved us, not because of righteous things we had done, but because of his mercy." God wants us to offer that same mercy to those around us.

Discussion Questions
◎ When has someone shown you mercy?
◎ Can you think of someone who needs your forgiveness or help?

Prayer Prompter
Please help us to have mercy for others. Please have mercy on us.

Have Mercy!

Be Pure in Heart

Memory Verse
"Blessed are the pure in heart, for they will see God"
(Matthew 5:8).

Attention Grabber
Use tape to make the outline of a large heart on a windowpane or mirror. Have the kids think of something wrong they have done recently; then have them stick their index fingers into a spoonful of peanut butter and make smudges on the heart. As you tell them that God wants to wash our hearts completely pure and clean, spray window cleaner on the glass and wipe away the smudges. Emphasize that God can wash away our sins because Jesus took the punishment for us.

Living It
When we look into our hearts and see sin, we shouldn't ignore it and go on with life as usual. We need for God to wash our hearts. God promises to make our hearts pure (completely clean) if we ask him. "If we confess our sins, he is faithful and just and will forgive us our sins and purify us from all unrighteousness" (1 John 1:9). David prayed, "Search me, O God, and know my heart; test me and know my anxious thoughts. See if there is any offensive way in me, and lead me in the way everlasting" (Psalm 139:23, 24).

Discussion Questions
◉ Does God want us to stay away from him for a while after we sin? (No! He wants us to repent right away.)
◉ Is there anything in your heart you wouldn't want God to see?

Prayer Prompter
Please search our hearts and make them pure.

Be a Peacemaker
Matthew 5:9

Memory Verse
"Blessed are the peacemakers, for they will be called sons of God"
(Matthew 5:9).

Attention Grabber
Let the kids choose "heads" or "tails" and toss a coin. Mention that some people toss a coin to solve simple problems. Ask what are some other ways to solve problems. Which ways are good? (talking calmly, compromise). Which are bad? (taking what you want, yelling).

Living It
If a stick of dynamite were about to explode, you could stop it by pulling out the fuse (although you shouldn't try it!). Situations arise almost every day that could cause us or others to explode with anger. We can defuse those situations by answering with kindness. God wants us to be peacemakers like that. Then people will know that we're God's children.

If a fire wasn't stopped, it could burn a home, a neighborhood, and eventually a whole nation. Anger, like a fire, can destroy a home, a neighborhood, and a nation. Criticism, teasing, name-calling, yelling, and arguing make anger grow like pouring gasoline on a fire. Proverbs 15:1 says "A gentle answer turns away wrath, but a harsh word stirs up anger."

Discussion Questions
- What is a recent example of when you (not anyone else) stirred up anger in someone in our family?
- How could you have been more of a peacemaker?

Prayer Prompter
Please help us to be peacemakers in our family and in the world.

Persecuted People
Matthew 5:10-12

Memory Verse

"Blessed are those who are persecuted because of righteousness, for theirs is the kingdom of heaven" (Matthew 5:10).

Attention Grabber

Have the kids name stories in which the main character is mistreated but there is a happy ending, such as *Cinderella, The Wizard of Oz,* and *The Ugly Duckling.* Explain that in real life sometimes we will be mistreated for following Jesus, but we know we have a happy ending ahead of us.

Living It

It's hard to understand, but some people will treat us badly simply because we try to follow Jesus. They may tease us because we won't do things they do. In some places, people kill Christians or put them in prison for following Christ. We can't let this discourage us or make us hide our faith. We may be persecuted for our faith (see Matthew 5:11, 12), but we need to remember the happy ending—we'll go to be with God in heaven!

Discussion Questions

- Why would the devil like for us to be afraid to tell others about our faith?
- How have you responded when people have teased you about trying to follow Jesus?

Prayer Prompter

Please keep our faith strong and help us to stand up for you even when others put us down for it.

Stay Salty
Matthew 5:13

Memory Verse
"You are the salt of the earth. But if the salt loses its saltiness, how can it be made salty again? It is no longer good for anything, except to be thrown out and trampled by men" (Matthew 5:13).

Attention Grabber
Serve a food you usually salt (such as boiled eggs or popcorn). But this time, leave the food unsalted. Who noticed the difference?

Living It
We use salt to improve the taste of food. Jesus wants to use us to improve the world. He wants us to stay "salty"—full of faith, and enthusiastic about his good news. Then our lives make noticeable improvements in the world.

Discussion Questions
- What can we tell others about Jesus that will make their lives better?
- What are situations in which God can use your life to improve the world now, and later when you're grown?

Prayer Prompter
Please use us to improve the world. Please help us grow in our faith and enthusiasm for you.

Light of the World
Matthew 5:14

Memory Verse
"You are the light of the world. A city on a hill cannot be hidden"
(Matthew 5:14).

Attention Grabber
Show the difference between a glow-in-the-dark object (such as a wristwatch or toy) in the light and in the darkness. Emphasize that we may not think our influence on others is very noticeable, but because the world is a dark place, the light makes a big difference.

Living It
When we spend time with God in prayer and Bible study, he fills us with his love and peace. It is like being poured full of light. People notice that. Some express that by saying, "I see Jesus in you!" or "You just have a glow about you!" Picture yourself as a lighthouse with the love of God shining out to others and helping them find their way.

Discussion Questions
◉ What could happen to ships in a harbor if there wasn't a light-house?
◉ How can we be a light to others?

Prayer Prompter
Please shine through us to help others find their way to you.

Don't Hide Your Light
Matthew 5:15

Memory Verse
"Neither do people light a lamp and put it under a bowl. Instead they put it on its stand, and it gives light to everyone in the house" *(Matthew 5:15).*

Attention Grabber
Light a votive candle and then place a bowl over it. Or light a birthday candle and place a ceramic mug over it. Ask the children: Can the flame brighten anyone's life under there? What happens to the flame? If we hide our faith, does it help others? What happens to our faith?

Living It
A lamp couldn't fulfill its purpose under a bowl. We can't fulfill our purpose if we hide our faith. To let God use us the way he wants, we need to be open about our faith and love people like he does. That way God can shine through our loving actions.

Discussion Questions
◎ Are there any "bowls" in our lives—any ways we have tried to hide our faith?
◎ How can you give light to others in our house this week?

Prayer Prompter
Please give us the courage to let our faith burn brightly for others to see.

Let Your Light Shine
Matthew 5:16

Memory Verse
"In the same way, let your light shine before men, that they may see your good deeds and praise your Father in heaven" (Matthew 5:16).

Attention Grabber
Take apart a couple of cheap flashlights and let the kids race to reassemble them. Emphasize that we are like flashlights and the Holy Spirit is like the batteries. He gives us the ability to love others like God does. We need to let the light shine out of us by being kind and loving to others.

Living It
If people see our kindness and love but don't know we're Christians, they will mistakenly give the honor to us instead of Jesus. It's important to let them know that the love we show them is only a small portion of the love that God has for them. We need to let them know that his Holy Spirit enables us to do what God wants.

Discussion Questions
- What is something you can do for someone today that will help him or her feel God's love?
- How can we "get connected" with the Holy Spirit?

Prayer Prompter
Please show us how you want to reach out to others through us. Please help others to praise you when they see the good we do.

Jesus and the Law
Matthew 5:17, 18

Memory Verse

"Do not think that I have come to abolish the Law or the Prophets; I have not come to abolish them but to fulfill them" (Matthew 5:17).

Attention Grabber

Have the kids each tear out an illustration from a magazine that depicts a real object that you have on hand (for example, a picture of a banana and a real banana or a picture of a pet and your real pet). Put the illustrations and the objects side by side. Emphasize that these illustrations are "pictures" of the real thing. God's laws, such as the Ten Commandments, are a picture of what God wants us to be like. They are a picture of Jesus.

Living It

Jesus came to fulfill God's law. That means he came to obey all of it, to keep the promises the prophets made about him, and to show for real how we should live. Jesus was the only person who could keep all of the commandments. Galatians 3:24 says the law was a "schoolmaster to bring us unto Christ" *(King James Version)*. The commandments are teachers that show us how much we need Jesus. They show us that no matter how good our actions are, our actions can never be good enough for us to deserve heaven. James 2:10 says that "whoever keeps the whole law and yet stumbles at just one point is guilty of breaking all of it." That is why we need Jesus as our Savior, to save us from the punishment we deserve for being unable to keep the commandments.

Discussion Question

◉ What are some of the commandments and how did Jesus obey them?

Prayer Prompter

Thank you for sending your Son to fulfill your law. Help us to live like him and to have faith in him as our Savior.

Not Righteous Enough

Memory Verse

"For I tell you that unless your righteousness surpasses that of the Pharisees and the teachers of the law, you will certainly not enter the kingdom of heaven" (Matthew 5:20).

Attention Grabber

Have the kids pat themselves on the back. Explain that the Pharisees were people who were always "patting themselves on the back"—feeling very proud of themselves for all of their good deeds. They thought they were so good they didn't need forgiveness.

Living It

Jesus said that to enter heaven, people had to be more right with God than the Pharisees and teachers of the law. They were known for outwardly being sticklers about even the tiniest commandments, but their hearts were full of wrong thoughts. Jesus said to them, "You have neglected the more important matters of the law—justice, mercy and faithfulness" (Matthew 23:23). He told a story in which he compared a proud Pharisee who bragged about his good deeds in his prayers and a tax collector who humbly begged God to forgive his sins. Jesus said the tax collector was the one who was right with God (Luke 18:9-14). God wants us to try to obey him, but also to recognize how much we need his forgiveness. We can't keep every commandment, which is what would be required for us to deserve heaven on our own.

Discussion Questions

◉ What are motives? (The reasons in our hearts for our actions.)
◉ What are some wrong motives for doing the right thing?

Prayer Prompter

Help us to stay humble, remembering how merciful you are to forgive us. Thank you for making us right with you through Jesus' sacrifice.

Don't Call Names
Matthew 5:22

Memory Verse
"Anyone who says, 'You fool!' will be in danger of the fire of hell"
(Matthew 5:22).

Attention Grabber
Pretend to throw a ridiculously childish temper tantrum. Ask if that is the way God wants us to feel and act.

Living It
The Old Testament said not to murder. Jesus said that actually God's law extends beyond that. It's a sin to even *want* to murder someone. God doesn't want us to stay angry at people or call them names. In fact, Jesus said, "But anyone who says, 'You fool!' will be in danger of the fire of hell." Ephesians 4:26 says, "Do not let the sun go down while you are still angry."

Discussion Questions
◉ What are good ways to get over feeling angry?
◉ What are bad ways to get over feeling angry?

Prayer Prompter
Please help us not to be angry with anyone. Help us to forgive quickly.

Make Up First

Memory Verse

"Therefore, if you are offering your gift at the altar and there remember that your brother has something against you, leave your gift there in front of the altar. First go and be reconciled to your brother; then come and offer your gift" (Matthew 5:23, 24).

Attention Grabber

Place a stuffed animal (preferably a lamb or a bull) on a fireplace hearth or on a small table. Explain that in Bible times people brought animals and other offerings to be burned on a table, called an altar, for the forgiveness of their sins and to express thanks.

Living It

We no longer need to sacrifice animals because Jesus "gave himself up for us as a fragrant offering and sacrifice to God" (Ephesians 5:2); but these verses apply to any time we want to do something that will please God. He doesn't want us to love just him; he wants us to love his children, too. First John 4:21 says, "And he has given us this command: Whoever loves God must also love his brother." Before we do "good works," we need to make sure no one has any reason to be angry because of a wrong thing we've done.

Discussion Questions

⊚ Can you think of anyone who is angry with you?
⊚ What can you do to help people forgive you?

Prayer Prompter

Please help us to notice when others have bad feelings toward us. Show us what we can do to help them forgive us.

Settle Matters Quickly
Matthew 5:25, 26

Memory Verse
"Settle matters quickly with your adversary who is taking you to court. Do it while you are still with him on the way" (Matthew 5:25).

Attention Grabber
Shake a can of soda once and ask, "If I were going to pour this into a glass for you, would you want me to let this settle or keep shaking it?" Continue shaking the can and then open it outdoors where it is OK for the soda to spew. Explain that people are a little like this. It is better to help them get over their anger right away than it is to let it bubble up until they "explode."

Living It
Jesus said to try to settle disagreements and pay our debts quickly. Sometimes the longer we wait, the worse things get. If we don't solve problems with people right away, their annoyance could turn into a grudge and they might even try to get revenge.

Discussion Questions
◎ What are some disagreements you have settled well?
◎ What did you do and say that helped to calm everyone?

Prayer Prompter
Please help us to resolve disagreements quickly.

Don't Lust
Matthew 5:27, 28

Memory Verse
"You have heard that it was said, 'Do not commit adultery.' But I tell you that anyone who looks at a woman lustfully has already committed adultery with her in his heart" (Matthew 5:27, 28).

Attention Grabber
Note to parents: Even if discussing sex with your children makes you or them uncomfortable, your children need to hear from you now the truth about God's plan for sex, or later they may not want to hear the truth at all. Make a fake "apple pie" by pouring water, cinnamon, and a few cloves into a saucepan. Heat. Let the aroma waft through your home until at least one family member comes to see what smells so good. Explain that the fake apple pie scent is a little like lust. The devil lures people toward an experience that will bring disappointment because it is not the real thing. It doesn't bring happiness like love expressed between people who are committed to each other enough to marry.

Living It
The Bible says that it is wrong for anyone to have sex with someone who isn't the person's husband or wife. Jesus said it's just as wrong for people to think about doing that. This is called lusting. That is one of the reasons it is wrong to look at magazines, internet sites, television shows, or movies in which characters are not wearing enough clothes or are having sex. That is also why God wants us to dress modestly—so we won't cause others to feel that way toward us.

Discussion Questions
◉ Why is married sex good, but adultery and lust are wrong?
◉ What can you do if you're at someone else's house and an inappropriate show comes on TV?

Prayer Prompter
Please keep our minds and actions pure.

Get Rid of Sin
Matthew 5:29, 30; 18:8, 9; Mark 9:43-48

Memory Verse
"And if your right hand causes you to sin, cut it off and throw it away. It is better for you to lose one part of your body than for your whole body to go into hell" (Matthew 5:30).

Attention Grabber
Turn an oversized, long-sleeved shirt inside out and tie a knot in the end of the right sleeve. Then turn the shirt right-side out and wear it. Read the Bible verse and show your "missing" hand.

Living It
Jesus doesn't want people to hurt themselves physically. He used the examples of an eye and a hand because they are parts of our bodies that are very important to us and would be painful to lose. Also, often what our eyes see and what our hands want to own or hold can tempt us. He was trying to show that it is extremely important to get temptations out of our lives, even if it is painful to lose them. For example, it might be very painful to give up a relationship in which your friend is causing you to sin, but your relationship with God is much more important.

Discussion Questions
◉ What did Joseph leave behind so he could escape from Potiphar's wife? (See Genesis 39.)
◉ Think of a sin you keep repeating. What do you need to leave behind so you won't be tempted anymore?

Prayer Prompter
Please help us to get rid anything that causes us to sin.

Memory Verse
"But I tell you that anyone who divorces his wife, except for marital unfaithfulness, cause her to become an adulteress, and anyone who marries the divorced woman commits adultery" (Matthew 5:32).

Attention Grabber
Look at wedding pictures of a happily married couple (yours, grandparents', or friends'). If possible, look at pictures from the same couple's tenth, twenty-fifth, or fiftieth anniversary.

Living It
When people marry, God joins them together. He doesn't want anyone or anything to tear the couple apart (Matthew 19:4-6). "Marital unfaithfulness" is when a husband or a wife has a sexual relationship with someone else. This is called "adultery." Jesus said that is a reason that one spouse may divorce the other. We can't look at people who are divorced and judge their reasons. Just decide that if you get married, you will do all that you can to keep your own marriage strong. If your friends have parents who are divorced, be loving and supportive. Don't criticize or make fun of them.

Discussion Question
◉ What are some ways you can prepare to have a strong, divorce-proof marriage? (Choose your spouse prayerfully and carefully; learn to get along with others now so you can get along with your spouse; understand that marriage is permanent; resist sexual temptations before and during marriage.)

Prayer Prompter
If we get married, please help our marriages to stay strong. Please prevent the divorce of couples we know who are having trouble. Please heal the pain caused by divorces among people we care about.

Don't Swear
Matthew 5:33-37

Memory Verse

"And do not swear by your head, for you cannot make even one hair white or black. Simply let your 'Yes' be 'Yes,' and 'No,' 'No'; anything beyond this comes from the evil one" (Matthew 5:36, 37).

Attention Grabber

Ask the kids if they have ever heard a "bleep" on television when someone said a bad word. Tell the kids that in the 1960s and earlier, one of the expressions that would have been replaced by a bleep was "I swear."

Living It

Do you hear people say, "I swear" often? God doesn't want us to use holy language casually like that. By swearing, people are saying that their promise is so serious that they'll let something terrible happen to them if they break it. That overly proud attitude is offensive to God because he is really the one who is in control. We may be able to use dye to change the color of our hair, but we don't have the power to make it grow a different color. We don't have control over everything that happens, but God is so powerful that he can do anything.

Discussion Questions

- ◉ Don't answer aloud, but ask yourself, "Are there any words or expressions I say that may offend God?"
- ◉ Talk about words (particularly euphemisms) that may not be "swear" words, but may not please God. What are some of them? Why shouldn't we say them?

Prayer Prompter

Help us to use only language that honors you.

Don't Swear

Turn the Other Cheek

Memory Verse

"But I tell you, Do not resist an evil person. If someone strikes you on the right cheek, turn to him the other also" (Matthew 5:39).

Attention Grabber

Beforehand, rub blush or lipstick on your hands and pat your hands against your cheeks so the handprints clearly show. Then clean your hands. Before reading today's story, can the kids guess what the memory verse is? Wipe off the handprints and continue with the devotion.

Living It

When people try to fight us, it is natural to want to fight back. But that's not how God wants us to react. Jesus says to forgive and let people have another chance. God doesn't want us to repay evil for evil (Romans 12:17, 18). Romans 12:18 says, "If it is possible, as far as it depends on you, live at peace with everyone."

Some people are mean because that's the way they've always been treated. Your kindness may be the first time anyone has ever been nice to them. You can show them how God feels about them. The world may think it's cowardly not to fight back; but actually, it takes great courage.

Discussion Questions

◉ What are some situations in which you have been treated unfairly?

◉ How would Jesus want you to react?

Prayer Prompter

Help us to resist the temptation to fight back and get revenge.

Give Your Cloak
Matthew 5:40

Memory Verse

"And if someone wants to sue you and take your tunic, let him have your cloak as well" (Matthew 5:40).

Attention Grabber

Wear a nightgown and robe that resemble Bible-times attire. Explain that a tunic was the piece of clothing that looked like a dress and the cloak looked like a coat. Explain that suing someone means taking him to a courtroom to try to get a judge to force that person to give you something.

Living It

Have you heard the expression, "He would give you the shirt off his back?" That refers to a person who is so full of love and generosity that he would give away something he genuinely needs. Jesus wants us to be that way, even to people who try to force us to give them our belongings. He wants us to treat people like they matter more than our belongings. In fact, he wants us to give them more than they are trying to take!

Discussion Questions

◎ What are some recent situations in which you could have "kept the peace" by giving someone a material possession?
◎ What do you have that it would be hard to share or give away?

Prayer Prompter

Help us to remember that people matter more than things. Help us to be generous even with people who try to take things from us.

Go the Extra Mile
Matthew 5:41

Memory Verse
"If someone forces you to go one mile, go with him two miles"
(Matthew 5:41).

Attention Grabber
If you can, talk about today's verse while taking a two-mile walk. Explain that in Bible times, the king's couriers (who carried mail, information, or supplies) could force citizens to help them for one mile. Jesus said to do more than we are forced to do. If you can't go for a walk, explain that the expression "bend over backward" means to do more than is comfortable to help people. Let the children literally bend over backward to do the limbo under a broom while music plays.

Living It
When people make us do things, we might feel like complaining. But if we think of the work as serving God, it helps us to want to do a great job. Colossians 3:23 says, "Whatever you do, work at it with all your heart, as working for the Lord, not for men." Jesus said that when you are forced to do something, instead of complaining about it, do twice as much. When you don't complain and you do more than asked, you show love to the people who needed your help.

Discussion Questions
◎ What are some extra things you could do beyond your normal responsibilities?
◎ How would these help you and other people?

Prayer Prompter
Help us to have a willing attitude toward those who make us work. Help us to show love by doing even more than people expect from us.

Give and Lend
Matthew 5:42

Memory Verse
"Give to the one who asks you, and do not turn away from the one who wants to borrow from you" (Matthew 5:42).

Attention Grabber
Call a homeless shelter or food bank to find out their hours. Your church may be able to put you in contact with one. Have the kids help you pack a bag of groceries to take to a food pantry or make sandwiches to give to homeless people. Ask how the children feel when they know they are helping others.

Living It
Sharing with people in need can give you a great feeling. In fact, there isn't a more rewarding way to spend money than to help someone who is in trouble. Jesus doesn't want us to ignore the problems of other people or refuse to help them. He wants us to show love by sharing what we have. If you were in need and you mustered the courage to ask for help, how would you feel if someone turned you away? God doesn't want us to treat people that way.

Discussion Questions
- Which charities receive contributions from our family?
- Can you remember a situation in which you or our whole family gave to someone in need?

Prayer Prompter
Help us to show love by sharing with others.

Love and Greet Everyone

Memory Verse

"If you love those who love you, what reward will you get? Are not even the tax collectors doing that? And if you greet only your brothers, what are you doing more than others? Do not even pagans do that?" (Matthew 5:46, 47).

Attention Grabber

How many different waves can everyone in the family do? (beauty queen, high five, low five, Star Trek Vulcan "live long and prosper," etc.) Explain that God doesn't want us to just be friendly and loving to those who are nice to us. He wants us to greet and show kindness to everyone.

Living It

Do you ever wait to see how people feel about you before deciding whether to like them? God doesn't do that. He makes the sun rise on the good and the bad. He sends rain to both. He loves all people, whether they love him or not. He wants us to be that way, too.

Discussion Questions

- How could you cheer the grumpiest person you know today? (smile, tell a joke, give a flower or treat, etc.)
- Who has been kind to us even when we were mean and grumpy?

Prayer Prompter

Help us reach out to people who haven't reached out to us.

Let God Perfect You
Matthew 5:48

Memory Verse
"Be perfect, therefore, as your heavenly Father is perfect"
(Matthew 5:48).

Attention Grabber
Give everyone a piece of clay to mold (or see page 265 for a simple bread clay recipe) or show a pot, pitcher, or sculpture made from clay. Isaiah 64:8 says, "Yet, O Lord, you are our Father. We are the clay, you are the potter; we are all the work of your hand."

Living It
"We are God's workmanship" (Ephesians 2:10) and he is gradually making us more like Jesus (Romans 8:29). Don't be discouraged if it takes a while for him to finish perfecting you. He will be faithful to complete what he started in you (Philippians 1:6). Someday when we see Jesus, we will be like him (1 John 3:2, 3). The way to become like him in this world is to love others (1 John 4:16, 17). If you stay flexible and let God transform you as he wants to do, he will perfect you.

Discussion Questions
◎ What ways has God made our family members more like Jesus as time has passed?
◎ How can you be more like Jesus?

Prayer Prompter
Help us to obey when you try to help us improve.

Serve Secretly
Matthew 6:1

Memory Verse

"Be careful not to do your 'acts of righteousness' before men, to be seen by them. If you do, you will have no reward from your Father in heaven" (Matthew 6:1).

Attention Grabber

Give everyone some star stickers, if you have them. Have one family member shine a lamp on you as if it is a spotlight. Go into the spotlight and pretend to shine someone else's shoe. At the same time another person should pretend to shine a shoe out of the spotlight without calling attention to himself or herself. Encourage everyone to put stars on you and tell you what a good job you did. Ask which of you—the person inside or outside the spotlight—served others the way God wants us to do.

Living It

When we do kind things secretly, it helps to keep our motives pure. When no one will find out, we do nice things because we love God and other people, not to receive praise and admiration. God wants to reward us when we do good things for the right reasons. If we do them for people's praise, that is the only reward we will receive.

Discussion Question

◉ Why is it tempting to tell other people when we have done something nice?

Prayer Prompter

Please help us to resist bragging when we serve others.

Don't Toot Your Horn
Matthew 6:2

Memory Verse
"So when you give to the needy, do not announce it with trumpets, as the hypocrites do in the synagogues and on the streets, to be honored by men. I tell you the truth, they have received their reward in full" (Matthew 6:2).

Attention Grabber
Have a family member sit on the floor holding out a cup like a beggar. Walk up to him, pull out a toy trumpet or kazoo (see page 264 for directions), play a tune like you are announcing royalty, drop a coin in the cup, play "ta da" on the kazoo, and take several bows.

Living It
God wants us to be sensitive to the needs of others and help them. Proverbs 19:17 says, "He who is kind to the poor lends to the Lord, and he will reward him for what he has done." The virtuous woman described in Proverbs 31:20 "opens her arms to the poor and extends her hands to the needy." But God doesn't want us to help so we can get praise from others.

Discussion Questions
◎ What are ways we "toot our own horns"?
◎ How can we give without other people knowing it?

Prayer Prompter
Please help us to be quietly generous.

Don't Tell Your Left Hand

Memory Verse

"But when you give to the needy, do not let your left hand know what your right hand is doing, so that your giving may be in secret. Then your Father, who sees what is done in secret, will reward you" (Matthew 6:3, 4).

Attention Grabber

Make hand puppets by drawing eyes on your fists and using your thumbs as mouths. Have one hand ramble on about how much it has done for others. Have the other one simply say, "Oh brother!"

Living It

Jesus wants us to be so quiet about the good we do that even we ourselves barely know it. He doesn't want us to dwell on our good actions in our conversations with others or even in our own thoughts. Otherwise we risk becoming proud about our own goodness. And the more we think about the good we do, the more likely it is that we will slip and brag about it. If one part of you doesn't think about what the other part of you has done, you might do twice as much!

Discussion Questions

◉ Do you know someone whose family may be struggling financially and may need our help?

◉ How can we help them secretly?

Prayer Prompter

Please show us who you want us to help, and give us the self-control to keep quiet about it.

Showy Spirituality
Matthew 6:5, 6

Memory Verse

"But when you pray, go into your room, close the door and pray to your Father, who is unseen. Then your Father, who sees what is done in secret, will reward you" (Matthew 6:6).

Attention Grabber

Beforehand, gather several Bibles and cut the center out of a paper plate to make a "halo." During the devotion, pretend that leaders from your church will be coming for a visit. Set out the Bibles in prominent spots. Place the halo on your head and say, "I wonder if I should spray paint my halo gold or add some glitter?" Point to a bare spot on the wall and say, "I wonder if I have time to needlepoint Bible verses before they get here?" Then ask your family what you were trying to do (impress others with your spirituality). Ask "Was that right?"

Living It

Religious leaders in Jesus' time were trying to impress people with their spirituality by praying in the street. God wants us to have a sincere relationship with him that is not just for show. If our only relationship with God is limited to the prayer and study we do in church, we will not have a very deep relationship with him. He wants us to spend time alone with him, too.

Discussion Questions

- What kinds of things would you pray about one-on-one with God that you might not pray in public?
- How can we share our faith without bragging about it?

Prayer Prompter

Please help us not to show off about our relationship with you. Remind us to spend one-on-one time in prayer with you every day.

Showy Spirituality

Pray From Your Heart

Memory Verse

"And when you pray, do not keep on babbling like pagans, for they think they will be heard because of their many words. Do not be like them, for your Father knows what you need before you ask him" *(Matthew 6:7, 8).*

Attention Grabber

Tell the kids cute ways they mispronounced words when they were learning to talk. Then explain that babbling is talk that is meaningless, such as babies do before they learn to talk.

Living It

Some people chant sounds or words again and again, thinking that will get God's attention. Sometimes people use long, fancy, meaningless phrases to make their prayers sound impressive. God wants us to pray simply and sincerely from our hearts. Jesus gave us the Model Prayer (Matthew 6:9-13) as an example to teach us the kinds of things God wants us to pray.

Discussion Questions

- Are there phrases you've said so many times in your prayers that you don't even think about what they mean? What are they?
- How can you mean what you say?

Prayer Prompter

Help us to pray sincerely from our hearts.

Worship God's Holiness

Matthew 6:9

Memory Verse

"This, then, is how you should pray: 'Our Father in heaven, hallowed be your name'" (Matthew 6:9).

Attention Grabber

Sing a worship song such as "Holy, Holy, Holy" together.

Living It

We need to worship God in our prayers, not to just rush into our "gimmee-gimmee" list. If we picture God in heaven, it can inspire awe for his holiness. "Hallowed" means holy, completely good, and free from all evil. Isn't it amazing that the God of the whole universe loves you personally and cares for you as a father does? He adopted you as his child when you believed in Jesus (Ephesians 1:5). Because of Jesus, we can approach our Father's throne with confidence, and he'll give us mercy and grace when we're in need (Hebrews 4:15, 16).

Discussion Questions

- What are some times when you have been especially awed by God's holiness?
- What kinds of words can you use to worship God?

Prayer Prompter

Thank you for being a perfect Father to us.

Your Will Be Done

Matthew 6:10

Memory Verse

"Your kingdom come, your will be done on earth as it is in heaven"
(Matthew 6:10).

Attention Grabber

Have the kids draw angels. They can put wings on the angels by tracing around their hands. Have them write "Help Me Obey Like the Angels Do" under the picture.

Living It

God wants us to pray for the whole world, not just for our own lives. Look at the big picture. Pray that everyone will accept him as their king. Pray that everyone, starting with you yourself, will obey God the way he is obeyed in heaven.

Discussion Question

◎ Can you think of a way you need to obey God better?

Prayer Prompters

Please help the world to accept you as king. Help us all to do your will the way the angels do in heaven.

Our Daily Bread
Matthew 6:11

Memory Verse
"Give us today our daily bread" (Matthew 6:11).

Attention Grabber
Have the kids write today's verse around the edges of paper plates. Then put a slice of hot bread on each of their plates. It could be quick bread from a mix, a thawed and baked loaf from frozen dough, canned rolls, a loaf from a bread machine, or even French bread hot from the grocery store bakery.

Living It
God wants us to express our need for his care. All of our food, clothing, shelter, and every other blessing in our life come from him. Sometimes it's easy to rush through the prayer at mealtime when the food smells so good, but let's take time to focus on sincere gratitude that God has given the food to us.

Discussion Questions
- Let's do a little detective work to trace how our food comes from God. Who bought the bread or ingredients?
- Where did that person get the money?
- Who blessed that person with the job where he or she earned the money?
- Who helped the farmers grow the food?

Prayer Prompter
Please bless us with the food we need today as you have in the past. Help us to appreciate always how well you take care of us.

Our Daily Bread

Forgiven Debts
Matthew 6:12; Luke 11:4

Memory Verse

"Forgive us our debts, as we also have forgiven our debtors"
(Matthew 6:12).

Attention Grabber

Beforehand, make a simple I.O.U. note for each family member promising a back rub or small favor. Explain that when people owe others something, sometimes they write "I.O.U." to say that they plan to pay their debt.

Living It

A debt is something you owe someone else. When others wrong us, we might feel that they owe us an apology or that they need to make it up to us before we will forgive them. God has given us an overwhelming amount of forgiveness through his grace. Colossians 3:13 says to "Forgive as the Lord forgave you." When we think about how much God has forgiven us, that makes it easier to forgive others. God will help us to forgive others if we ask him.

Discussion Questions

◉ Think of someone who has done something wrong to you. If you had sinned against that person instead, would you want that person and God to forgive you, even if you didn't deserve it?
◉ Who can you forgive for something they "owe" you?

Prayer Prompter

Please help us to forgive everyone. Please forgive us.

Deliver Us From Evil
Matthew 6:13

Memory Verse

"And lead us not into temptation, but deliver us from the evil one"
(Matthew 6:13).

Attention Grabber

Show the kids fishing lures and emphasize how much they look like the real thing. (Borrow from a neighbor who fishes if you don't have any.) Explain that as a fish is on its way to search for real food, it may get tricked into biting this fake food. Then the fish is in big trouble! The devil tries to lure us off the path of following Jesus. His temptations look good, but they only lead to trouble and disappointment.

Living It

James 1:13, 14 says, "When tempted, no one should say, 'God is tempting me.' For God cannot be tempted by evil, nor does he tempt anyone; but each one is tempted when, by his own evil desire, he is dragged away and enticed." If we are following God's leading, we can spot temptation when it tries to lure us off the path. Throughout the day, listen for the Holy Spirit's guidance. When you are tempted, look for the way out of it that God has prepared for you. First Corinthians 10:13 promises that God "will not let you be tempted beyond what you can bear" and that "he will also provide a way out so that you can stand up under it."

Discussion Questions

- What kinds of things lead you to sin?
- Think of a temptation that keeps coming to you. What are the ways God is providing for you to keep from doing that sin again?

Prayer Prompter

Help us to follow you and not be led away into temptation. Help us see the ways that you provide for us to resist temptation.

Deliver Us From Evil

Forgive and Be Forgiven

Matthew 6:14, 15

Memory Verse

"For if you forgive men when they sin against you, your heavenly Father will also forgive you. But if you do not forgive men their sins, your Father will not forgive your sins" (Matthew 6:14, 15).

Attention Grabber

If you have kneadable erasers, let the kids stretch them out and form them into fun shapes on the end of pencils. Then have them draw scribbles or black clouds to represent sins others have done against them that they haven't forgiven. Next, have them draw other clouds to represent their sins they need for God to forgive. While they very slowly erase the clouds or scribbles, have each person pray silently for God to take the grudges and sins out of his or her heart.

Living It

We need God to erase sins every day. He wants to erase everything evil out of our hearts, including old grudges that have been sitting in there!

Discussion Question

◉ How have you been able to forgive someone who has hurt you in the past?

Prayer Prompter

Please erase the grudges out of our hearts. Please erase our sins.

Don't Brag About Fasting
Matthew 6:16-18

Memory Verse

"But when you fast, put oil on your head and wash your face, so that it will not be obvious to men that you are fasting." (Matthew 6:17).

Attention Grabber

Mess up your hair and let your face hang as if completely exhausted. Tell your stomach to quit growling. When a family member asks what's wrong with you, reply, "Isn't this how you're supposed to act when you're fasting?" Mention that the morning meal is called breakfast because it breaks the fast and ends the time of not eating.

Living It

Fasting means to go without food. Jesus fasted forty days and nights before starting his ministry, but most fasts only last one to three days. Some people don't drink anything at all while they are fasting from food, and some people drink juices or water. During a fast, people usually feel more aware of God's presence because cravings for food remind them to pray. We shouldn't fast to get extra attention and praise from people for fasting, so that is why Jesus said to do it in secret. If children want to fast, they should always discuss it with their parents first.

Discussion Question

◉ What would be good reasons to fast? (To renew your focus on God, for help with an important decision, or for help with a serious problem.)

Prayer Prompter

Please help us know when to fast. Help us not to brag or complain when we fast.

Don't Brag About Fasting

Earthly Treasures
Matthew 6:19

Memory Verse

"Do not store up for yourselves treasures on earth, where moth and rust destroy, and where thieves break in and steal" (Matthew 6:19).

Attention Grabber

Look through a catalog together. Ask what will happen to the items you see in it as time passes.

Living It

When you've heard reporters interview a family who survived a tornado, fire, or other disaster, have you ever heard them say, "We lost everything"? That is a tragic situation, but if their family and faith are alive, they didn't lose what's most important. The material things in life are only temporary. God doesn't want us to waste our life being focused on things that won't last.

Discussion Questions

- Have you ever bought something that seemed very valuable until you got home and realized you didn't even need it?
- What is the most valuable thing you have?

Prayer Prompter

Free us from yearning for more and more belongings. Help us not to be materialistic. Help us to realize how temporary and meaningless most earthly possessions are, while taking good care of the blessings you've given us.

Heavenly Treasures
Matthew 6:20

Memory Verse

"But store up for yourselves treasures in heaven, where moth and rust do not destroy, and where thieves do not break in and steal" *(Matthew 6:20).*

Attention Grabber

Show your kids the obituary section of the newspaper. Explain what an obituary is if they don't know. Then pretend to read one as if it says the person "died with millions of dollars in several bank accounts, a yacht, two summer cottages, and a fleet of luxury cars." Ask, "Is that what will matter when we die? What will matter?"

Living It

The saying, "Whoever dies with the most toys wins!" is not true. None of our material belongings go with us. If we spend our life focused on money and what it can buy, we might waste our entire time on earth. The things that will last and that we will have with us in heaven are the love we have in our hearts, our memories, our faith, and people who have accepted Jesus. Our focus should be on our relationship with God and on telling others about Jesus' sacrifice for them so they can be with us in heaven. The things we buy won't be there.

Discussion Questions

- Who would you like to be with you in heaven?
- How can you help them learn about Jesus?
- How can we spend our money in ways that will have a lasting influence?

Prayer Prompter

Help us to put our energy, time, and money into what will still matter after we die.

Heavenly Treasures

Where Is Your Heart?

Matthew 6:21

Memory Verse

"For where your treasure is, there your heart will be also"
(Matthew 6:21).

Attention Grabber

Cut a poster board or other large piece of paper into a treasure chest shape. If you have an ink pad, let the kids use their index fingers to make fingerprint hearts in the chest. (Or they can simply draw hearts or paste paper cutout hearts.) Then have them write names of people they care about on the hearts.

Living It

Whatever we value most is our treasure. We will love whatever we value most. God wants us to love and value what will last—other people and our relationships with him. We need to love people enough to tell them about Jesus so they can know the way to heaven.

Discussion Question

◉ What can we do if we have already told someone about Jesus and she wasn't interested? (Pray for her, try again when the Holy Spirit tells us the time is right, write her a heartfelt letter, etc.)

Prayer Prompter

Keep our hearts on what matters. Help us to love you and people, not possessions. Help us show our love by telling people that Jesus is the way to heaven.

The Birds and You
Matthew 6:25, 26

Memory Verse

"Therefore I tell you, do not worry about your life, what you will eat or drink; or about your body, what you will wear. Is not life more important than food, and the body more important than clothes? Look at the birds of the air; they do not sow or reap or store away in barns, and yet your heavenly Father feeds them. Are you not much more valuable than they?" (Matthew 6:25, 26).

Attention Grabber

Dim all the lights except one and make shadow pictures of birds on the wall. Or, if you have time, make a birdhouse together from a large milk carton (or carton that contained goldfish crackers) stapled shut and spray painted white. Just poke a hole in the top and loop a string through it (this allows you to hang up the birdhouse). Cut out an entrance doorway and poke a small twig beneath it for a perch.

Living It

We don't need to worry about what we will eat or wear. Jesus promises that God will provide for us. God wants us to trust him to take care of us. If God feeds the birds, surely he will do the same for us. Whenever we see birds, they can remind us that God will provide what we need, just as he does for them.

Discussion Question

◉ How does worrying show a lack of trust in God?

Prayer Prompter

Help us to rely on you, so we can think about more important things than what we'll eat and wear.

Worry Doesn't Help
Matthew 6:27; Luke 12:25, 26

Memory Verse
"Who of you by worrying can add a single hour to his life?"
(Matthew 6:27).

Attention Grabber
Ask each child to demonstrate something a worrier does (pace, bite nails, wrinkle brow, sigh, overeat, bite lip, pull out hair).

Living It
People worry about all kinds of things, but it usually doesn't change anything. No one has enough power to add an hour to his life, so why worry about it? God wants us to have faith that he will take care of us. The Bible says, "Cast all your anxiety on him because he cares for you" (1 Peter 5:7). Sometimes bad things happen, but they all work out for the best. Romans 8:28 says, "And we know that in all things God works for the good of those who love him, who have been called according to his purpose."

Discussion Question
◉ What was a situation in which you worried that something bad might happen but it didn't?

Prayer Prompter
Give us faith that no matter what happens, you will work things out for our good.

The Lilies and You
Matthew 6:28-32

Memory Verse

"And why do you worry about clothes? See how the lilies of the field grow. They do not labor or spin. Yet I tell you that not even Solomon in all his splendor was dressed like one of these" (Matthew 6:28, 29).

Attention Grabber

Give your kids each a blade of grass. Show them how to make it whistle by placing it between your thumbs and blowing through the gap between the knuckles. If flowers are available, place them between two pieces of waxed paper and press them inside a heavy book.

Living It

Even though some plants only last a short time, God goes to the trouble of creating them and taking care of them. When we look at the way God provides what his creations in nature need, we can remember that he provides what we need, too.

Discussion Questions

- Of all of God's creations that you have seen, which was the most beautiful?
- How does God care for you?

Prayer Prompter

Help us to trust you to care for us like you take care of your other creations.

Memory Verse
"But seek first his kingdom and his righteousness, and all these things will be given to you as well" (Matthew 6:33).

Attention Grabber
Put a snack in one of your pockets and a small piece of clothing in your other pocket. Play "Hide-and-Seek" with the kids. When they find you, remind them that seeking means "looking for." Explain that when they seek God, the other blessings come along, too. (Pull the food and clothing out of your pockets to demonstrate.)

Living It
God wants us to seek him more than anything else. If we are right with God, everything else we need will come along, too. Every day we need to spend time talking with God, listening to him, studying the Bible, and trying to help his kingdom grow by helping others get to know Jesus as Savior and Lord.

Discussion Question
◉ What things in our lives take our attention away from God?

Prayer Prompter
Please remind us every day to seek you.

Enough Trouble
Matthew 6:34

Memory Verse
"Therefore do not worry about tomorrow, for tomorrow will worry about itself. Each day has enough trouble of its own" (Matthew 6:34).

Attention Grabber
Have the kids write the memory verse on each of your wall calendars—underneath the picture, across the boxes that don't have dates (at the beginning or end of the month), or at the bottom of the calendar.

Living It
Our memory verse isn't saying we shouldn't make any plans. It's saying not to dread things that lie ahead. Joy is a "fruit" (product) of the Holy Spirit (Galatians 5:22), and worrying can steal your joy. It can make you feel like you have a problem that doesn't even exist yet. Don't worry about what you'll face in the future; trust that God will be there helping you just like he is today.

Discussion Question
◉ What worries about the future do you need to turn over to God?

Prayer Prompter
Please help us not to worry about the future.

Take the Plank Out
Matthew 7:3-5

Memory Verse

"Why do you look at the speck of sawdust in your brother's eye and pay no attention to the plank in your own eye?" (Matthew 7:3).

Attention Grabber

Show your family a splinter of wood and a plank (such as one on a deck) to compare. Let everyone write the verse on a piece of scrap lumber and set it in a windowsill or make "sawdust clay" while you talk (using the recipe on page 265).

Living It

It's easy to spot others' smallest flaws while overlooking our own gigantic ones. In fact, our own faults prevent us from seeing other people's situations clearly. Have you heard these expressions: "That's the pot calling the kettle black," "It takes one to know one," and "You're one to talk"? People say those because an accuser's faults are usually just as bad or worse than those of the person she's criticizing. We need to be honest with ourselves about our own shortcomings and work on them. People don't need our "constructive criticism" as much as we think they do.

Discussion Questions

- How do you feel when people criticize you? Do others feel that way when you criticize them?
- Would you prefer to take advice from someone whose fault was worse than yours or someone who had overcome the fault?

Prayer Prompter

Help us overlook others' flaws and work on improving ourselves instead.

Pearls to Pigs

Matthew 7:6

Memory Verse

"Do not give dogs what is sacred; do not throw your pearls to pigs. If you do, they may trample them under their feet, and then turn and tear you to pieces" (Matthew 7:6).

Attention Grabber

Let the kids briefly try to put a string of faux pearls or other costume jewelry on your pet dog. If you don't have a dog, have them draw a picture of a dog or pig wearing jewelry. Point out that animals don't appreciate the value of the jewelry.

Living It

Jesus compared the kingdom of God to an expensive pearl that a man sold everything to buy (Matthew 13:45, 46). There is nothing more valuable than knowing that Jesus is your way to heaven and that he wants to lead you as your king. But just as animals don't appreciate valuable jewelry, some people don't appreciate Jesus' valuable message. If someone rejects the good news, don't think that it is your fault. Maybe that person is not ready. You can pray for that person, and continue to show love.

Discussion Question

◉ How can you tell when people are ready to hear about Jesus? (They act interested and respectful when you begin to share about Jesus; they open up about their needs and problems; the Holy Spirit prompts you; they ask questions about what you believe, etc.)

Prayer Prompter

Please help us know what you want us to tell others about you.

Ask, Seek, Knock
Matthew 7:7, 8

Memory Verse

"Ask and it will be given to you; seek and you will find; knock and the door will be opened to you. For everyone who asks receives; he who seeks finds; and to him who knocks, the door will be opened" *(Matthew 7:7, 8).*

Attention Grabber

Sneak outside and knock on the front door. When your children answer it, come inside and play a variation of "Hide-and-Seek" called "Sardines". Only "It" hides. As each player finds "It," that player hides with "It." The last one who finds "It" can be the next "It." Emphasize that the more we seek God, the closer our relationship with him can get.

Living It

Knocking on our front door always gets our attention, doesn't it? Jesus always pays attention to us when we go to him. If we ask him for something, he gives it to us. If we look for him, he reveals more and more about himself. If we "knock on his door," he welcomes us.

Discussion Question

◉ What does God offer us if we knock on his door? (We can spend time with Jesus in prayer, become a part of God's kingdom, and someday be let into heaven.)

Prayer Prompter

Please help us to be faithful about asking, seeking, and knocking.

God Gives Good Gifts
Matthew 7:9-11

Memory Verse

"Which of you, if his son asks for bread, will give him a stone? Or if he asks for a fish, will give him a snake? If you, then, though you are evil, know how to give good gifts to your children, how much more will your Father in heaven give good gifts to those who ask him!" (Matthew 7:9-11).

Attention Grabber

Have the kids write the verse on rocks or paving stones.

Living It

How would you feel if you asked for a slice of bread and I put a rock on your plate? What if you wanted fish sticks and I served you cobra nuggets? I wouldn't treat you like that! When you ask for something, I try to give you what's good for you. God does the same thing!

Discussion Question

◎ Do you ask God for the things you need? Why or why not?

Prayer Prompter

Please help us to ask you for what we need and trust you to give us what's best for us.

Narrow Gate
Matthew 7:13, 14

Memory Verse
"Enter through the narrow gate. For wide is the gate and broad is the road that leads to destruction, and many enter through it. But small is the gate and narrow the road that leads to life, and only a few find it" (Matthew 7:13, 14).

Attention Grabber
Make a bicycle obstacle course with soda bottles and chalk. Emphasize that sometimes it's harder to stay on the "straight and narrow," but it's worth it to try. When we slip off the path and do wrong things, we can be forgiven because of Jesus, and he helps us get back on again.

Living It
Jesus is the gate (John 10:7-9) and the way (John 14:6). Unfortunately, most people won't choose to accept him and follow him. We can't base our beliefs and behaviors on the majority. Whenever you find yourself thinking or saying, "But everybody's doing it," instead ask, "WWJD?" (What Would Jesus Do?).

Discussion Question
◉ What are some ways followers of Jesus live differently than the rest of the world because they are on a different path?

Prayer Prompter
Please help us to trust Jesus as the gate and the way. Please help us live the way you want us to live.

Know by the Fruit

Matthew 7:15-20

Memory Verse

"Watch out for false prophets. They come to you in sheep's clothing, but inwardly they are ferocious wolves. By their fruit you will recognize them. Do people pick grapes from thornbushes, or figs from thistles?" (Matthew 7:15, 16).

Attention Grabber

Arrange grapes or another fruit among the leaves of a houseplant as a centerpiece. When the kids notice, explain that fruit grows on fruit trees and not on this particular plant. Give each family member a banana and have him write "By their fruit you will recognize them" on the peel. If you can, go for a short walk to identify different trees and point out how easy it would be to tell which were apple trees if you could see the apples on them.

Living It

Jesus is saying to be careful who you let teach you about him. Does that person have the fruit of the Spirit? Is that person loving, peaceful, patient, kind, good, faithful, gentle, and self-controlled? No one except Jesus is perfect, but we need to make sure that some of these fruit are in our teachers' lives or we might be following someone that we shouldn't.

Discussion Question

◉ What are some fruit you see in the lives of leaders at our church?

Prayer Prompter

Please help us to be careful about who we follow.

Know by the Fruit

Walk the Walk

Memory Verse

"Not everyone who says to me, 'Lord, Lord,' will enter the kingdom of heaven, but only he who does the will of my Father who is in heaven" (Matthew 7:21).

Attention Grabber

Show the kids how to do the Monkees walk, the moon walk, an Egyptian walk, the crab walk, or any other walks you know.

Living It

What do people mean when they say, "Don't just talk the talk; walk the walk"? Jesus doesn't want us to just say we follow him as Lord without our actions showing it. James 1:22 tells us, "Do not merely listen to the word, and so deceive yourselves. Do what it says." Jesus wants us to know him personally and follow his specific direction for our own lives. (See Matthew 7:23.)

Discussion Questions

- What are some things that you say are right to do, but you don't do them?
- How can we really get to know Jesus as our personal Lord rather than just as a character in a book? (Pray and listen. Let him guide us personally. Do what he says.)

Prayer Prompter

Please help us get to know Jesus well and to follow him as Lord.

House on the Rock
Matthew 7:24-27

Memory Verse

"Therefore everyone who hears these words of mine and puts them into practice is like a wise man who built his house on the rock" *(Matthew 7:24).*

Attention Grabber

Sing "The Wise Man Built His House Upon the Rock" and "On Christ the Solid Rock I Stand." If you have juice boxes, let the kids decorate them as houses by covering them with construction paper, taping on a triangle for a roof, and taping a large circle to the bottom of the box for a rock. Then have them write the verse on one side of the box. When they can recite the verse without looking, they can drink the juice.

Living It

As we make decisions in our lives, we need to base each choice on what Jesus has said. By doing so, we will build a stable life that won't fall apart when problems come. When storms try to tear us down, they won't destroy us. If we build our faith on the fact that Jesus is our way to heaven, we can weather anything.

Discussion Questions

- Can you name some of Jesus' commands?
- How does living according to these commands help us to make it through hard times?

Prayer Prompter

Please help us see the areas in which we need to obey you better. As we build our lives, remind us to make the decisions carefully and prayerfully. Help us to have faith to trust you as our rock, the one thing that doesn't shift.

House on the Rock

Why Are You So Afraid?

Matthew 8:23-27; Mark 4:37-41; Luke 8:22-25

Memory Verse

He replied, "You of little faith, why are you so afraid?" Then he got up and rebuked the winds and the waves, and it was completely calm (Matthew 8:26).

Attention Grabber

Fill a jar half full of vinegar and stir in a couple drops of blue food coloring. Then fill the remainder of the jar with salad oil. Shake the jar to show what the storm was like and then hold it still to show what happened when Jesus said, "Quiet! Be still!" After the devotional, add seasonings to the mixture and you can serve it as salad dressing.

Living It

When the disciples were afraid, they went to Jesus for help. That's exactly what we need to do when we're afraid. Jesus had the power to calm the storm and the sea; he has the power to take care of whatever frightens us, too. When you are troubled with fear, go to Jesus; he can calm you as he calmed the sea.

Discussion Questions

◉ What are your fears?
◉ How can trusting Jesus get rid of them?

Prayer Prompter

Please calm our fears and replace them with faith.

Get Up and Walk
Matthew 9:1-8

Memory Verse
Then he said to the paralytic, "Get up, take your mat and go home" *(Matthew 9:6).*

Attention Grabber
Have a child lie down on a blanket. Carry or drag the blanket by its corners. Ask the kids how they would feel about being lowered through a roof this way. Tell them the story of the paralyzed man and his friends (Matthew 9:1-8). Emphasize that the man and his four friends must have been desperate to get to Jesus.

Living It
How is being without Jesus like being paralyzed? (No one can go to heaven without him. No one can live the kind of life God wants without the Holy Spirit.) How did Jesus heal the paralyzed man physically? How did Jesus heal him spiritually?

Discussion Questions
- The man in the story was blessed with friends who were willing to do almost anything to help him get to Jesus. Which friends do you feel this way about?
- Can you tell them about Jesus?
- Can you invite them to come to church with us?

Prayer Prompter
Please help our friends begin their "walk" with you.

The Sick Need a Doctor

Matthew 9:10-13; Mark 2:14-17

Memory Verse

On hearing this, Jesus said, "It is not the healthy who need a doctor, but the sick" (Matthew 9:12).

Attention Grabber

Let the kids write the memory verse on small adhesive bandage strips.

Living It

Many people put off coming to Jesus because they think he won't want them if they aren't already good. That's not true! Romans 5:8 says, "But God demonstrates his own love for us in this: While we were still sinners, Christ died for us." Everyone has sinned (Romans 3:23). "If we claim to be without sin, we deceive ourselves and the truth is not in us" (1 John 1:8). Jesus wants to get rid of that sin for us. If we're sick, we don't wait until we're healthy to go to the doctor. People don't need to try to be sin free before coming to Jesus. After all, he is the only one who can get rid of sin.

Discussion Questions

◎ How is being guilty like being sick?
◎ How does Jesus make us well?

Prayer Prompter

Please help us and our friends to ask Jesus to take our sins away.

According to Your Faith

Matthew 9:27-31

Memory Verse
Then he touched their eyes and said, "According to your faith will it be done to you" (Matthew 9:29).

Attention Grabber
Play a game in which you point to a body part, and the family members raise their hands or ring a bell to be the first to tell the story about when Jesus healed that part. If your children aren't that familiar with these stories, give them Bibles and Scripture references and have them race to tell you which body part Jesus healed.

Eyes: Jesus put mud on blind man's eyes (John 9:1-12).
Mouth: Jesus loosed the tongue of man who couldn't talk (Mark 7:31-37).
Ear: Jesus reattached ear on the high priest's servant in the Garden of Gethsemane (Luke 22:49-51).
Spine: Jesus healed woman who was bent over 18 years (Luke 13:10-13).
Hand: Jesus healed shriveled hand on the Sabbath (Luke 6:6-10).
Legs and feet: Jesus healed man at pool of Bethesda (John 5:1-9), and man lowered through the roof (Mark 2:1-12).

Living It
When Jesus healed people, he often said it was because of their faith. Jesus told a man who asked for his son to be healed, "Everything is possible for him who believes." The man answered, "I do believe; help me overcome my unbelief!" (Mark 9:23, 24). If we ask him, God can increase our faith in his power to heal.

Discussion Question
◉ In what situation did God miraculously heal someone in our family, an acquaintance, or someone we read about?

Prayer Prompter
Please help us have faith in your power to heal.

According to Your Faith

Workers for the Harvest
Matthew 9:37, 38; Luke 10:2

Memory Verse
Then he said to his disciples, "The harvest is plentiful but the workers are few. Ask the Lord of the harvest, therefore, to send out workers into his harvest field" (Matthew 9:37, 38).

Attention Grabber
Give each family member a piece of fresh fruit. (A fruit none have tried before, such as star fruit or a pomegranate, would be especially interesting.) Point out that when this fruit was ripe and ready to harvest, someone needed to pick it. Make Easy Fruit Dip if you wish (See recipe on page 266).

Living It
Many people are ready to accept the good news about Jesus. They're just waiting for someone to tell them about him. Jesus wants us to pray for plenty of Christians to be willing to do that. Even if we're not full-time missionaries, we can help with the harvest. Jesus wants us to pray for more Christians to be willing to help with the harvest, too.

Discussion Question
◎ How can we help with the harvest?

Prayer Prompter
Please use us and other Christians to help with the harvest. Please call many people to serve you as missionaries.

Freely Give
Matthew 10:7, 8

Memory Verse
"As you go, preach this message: 'The kingdom of heaven is near.' Heal the sick, raise the dead, cleanse those who have leprosy, drive out demons. Freely you have received, freely give" (Matthew 10:7, 8).

Attention Grabber
Give each family member a glass of water. Have the kids take turns praising God for good things he has done for them and pouring a little water into a large pitcher. Emphasize that your family's pitcher is overflowing—your lives are overflowing with blessings. Tell them God wants your family to pour his blessings out to other people.

Living It
When we think about how much God has done for us, it is overwhelming. He wants us to praise him to others so they can turn to him and receive the same blessings in their lives. He has given to us freely, and he wants us to give to others freely. He wants us to bring the power of God into other people's lives.

Discussion Questions
- What material blessings and abilities has God given to you?
- How can you share those blessings and abilities with others?

Prayer Prompter
Help us show our gratitude to you by sharing what you have given us.

Eyes Wide Open

Memory Verse
"I am sending you out like sheep among wolves. Therefore be as shrewd as snakes and as innocent as doves" (Matthew 10:16).

Attention Grabber
Have a No-Blinking Contest. How long can each family member keep her eyes wide open? Mention that keeping your "eyes wide open" is an expression for being aware of ways others may try to take advantage of you or harm you.

Living It
Jesus wants us to be aware of the bad around us so we can keep it from harming us. Sometimes keeping ourselves away from evil takes some planning. If friends invite us to the movies, before we say "yes" we need to ask which one so we can decide whether it's right for us. If we're going to a party, we need to ask what videos they plan to watch and what else will happen. We need to make sure we spend time with people who build our faith rather than tear it down.

Discussion Questions
◉ What is the difference between "naive" and "innocent"? ("Naive" means you are unaware of evils. "Innocent" means you are aware of evils, but choose not to participate in them.)
◉ What are other situations in which we need to be especially shrewd yet stay innocent?

Prayer Prompter
Please help us to be aware of the evil around us and stay away from it.

God Is Strongest
Matthew 10:28

Memory Verse
"Do not be afraid of those who kill the body but cannot kill the soul. Rather, be afraid of the One who can destroy both soul and body in hell" (Matthew 10:28).

Attention Grabber
Have an arm-wrestling or thumb-wrestling match. Ask who is the strongest man in the world. Emphasize that God is even stronger.

Living It
Who is the strongest of anyone anywhere? (God). In fact, he is omnipotent. That means "all powerful." "If God is for us, who can be against us?" (Romans 8:31). It really doesn't matter who's against us, because God is stronger. No matter how powerful people are, no one's power even compares to God's. It is important that we care more about what God wants than what people want. No matter how hard people try to force you to do what's wrong, stay loyal to God!

Discussion Questions
◉ In what situations have you been forced to choose between following God and other people?
◉ Why was it worthwhile to follow God?

Prayer Prompter
Please help us to stay loyal to you, no matter how much others pressure us to do what's wrong.

God Knows All About You

Memory Verse

"And even the very hairs of your head are all numbered"
(Matthew 10:30).

Attention Grabber

Braid or comb a family member's hair while you talk. Or let the kids grow some green-haired friends. Simply draw faces on disposable coffee cups, fill with potting soil, plant grass seeds in the soil, and sprinkle with water daily.

Living It

God knows more about you than you even know about yourself. The number of hairs on your head changes every day, and God keeps track. Even the smallest details of your life are very important to him.

Discussion Question

◉ Have you ever felt you shouldn't talk to God about something because it was too small or unimportant?

Prayer Prompter

Please help us to remember that you care about every detail of our lives.

More Than Sparrows
Matthew 10:31

Memory Verse
"So don't be afraid; you are worth more than many sparrows"
(Matthew 10:31).

Attention Grabber
Let the kids use cookie cutters to cut shapes out of stale bread for the birds. If you want them to, they can also spread peanut butter on the shapes and dip them in birdseed. Arrange the shapes and scraps onto a plate and set it outside where you will be able to see the birds from your window as they arrive for a snack.

Living It
God cares about every creature, even very small birds. You're worth much more than they are, so of course you are of great value to God. Basing your self-esteem on how others treat you is unreliable, but you can count on God's love for you always to stay strong. Whenever you start to feel unimportant, remember how valuable you are to God.

Discussion Question
◉ What can you remember when you see a bird? (I'm worth even more to God.)

Prayer Prompter
Please help us to remember how important we are to you.

More Than Sparrows

Unashamed of Jesus
Matthew 10:32, 33; Mark 8:38; Luke 9:26

Memory Verse
"Whoever acknowledges me before men, I will also acknowledge him before my Father in heaven. But whoever disowns me before men, I will disown him before my Father in heaven" (Matthew 10:32, 33).

Attention Grabber
Show the kids a plain sheet of white paper. Tell them this is a picture of a rabbit in a snowstorm. Discuss the fact that when animals camouflage themselves, they blend in with their surroundings. Emphasize that it isn't good to be a camouflaged Christian. We shouldn't try to blend in so much that people can't tell that we love Jesus.

Living It
Imagine that you and your best friend walked up to a group of kids at school. If your friend pretended not to know you because he or she was embarrassed about you, how would you feel? Jesus wants us to be loyal friends to him no matter who is around. He isn't just with us when we pray; he is with us all of the time, and he wants us to act like it. In Luke 9:26 he said, "If anyone is ashamed of me and my words, the Son of Man will be ashamed of him when he comes in glory." Pleasing Jesus is more important than impressing other people. If we want Jesus to tell our Father in heaven about us, we need to tell other people about Jesus.

Discussion Questions
◎ Have you been trying to hide your relationship with Jesus?
◎ What are ways you can bring up Jesus in everyday conversations with friends?

Prayer Prompter
Please help us to be open with others about our relationship with you.

Love God the Most
Matthew 10:37

Memory Verse

"Anyone who loves his father or mother more than me is not worthy of me; anyone who loves his son or daughter more than me is not worthy of me" (Matthew 10:37).

Attention Grabber

Hand a tape measure or ruler to a family member and say, "Measure your heart." We can't measure our feelings that way, but we can measure them by comparing them to other feelings. Do you like ice cream more or less than spinach? Swimming more than bowling? Science fiction movies better than westerns? Emphasize that it helps us know how much we love God by comparing that feeling to how much we love our family.

Living It

Jesus wants us to love him even more than we love our family. That doesn't mean he wants us to love our family less; it means he wants us to increase our love for him. Even though it may be hard for you to feel more love for Jesus than your family right now, as your relationship with him grows over the years, you will see how faithful he is to love you and help you. Your love for him will grow very strong if you let it.

Discussion Question

◎ In what situations have you especially felt love for Jesus?

Prayer Prompter

Please help us to love you more than anything or anyone else.

Kindness Rewarded
Matthew 10:42; Mark 9:41

Memory Verse
"And if anyone gives even a cup of cold water to one of these little ones because he is my disciple, I tell you the truth, he will certainly not lose his reward" (Matthew 10:42).

Attention Grabber
Let the kids offer a cup of water or an inexpensive bottle of water for free to joggers, the postal carrier, and anyone else who comes by your home this afternoon or this weekend. Emphasize that in this verse water represents kindness and helpfulness.

Living It
When we help others, even in the smallest ways, God wants to reward us for it. We honor God when we do kind things for those who follow him. We are showing love to him by showing it to them. Also, God loves you so much that he will bless anyone who helps you!

Discussion Question
◉ What are some ways we can help our church leaders, Sunday school teachers, missionaries, and other people who love Jesus?

Prayer Prompter
Please help us to be aware of ways we can help those who love you.

Tell the News!
Matthew 11:4, 5

Memory Verse

Jesus replied, "Go back and report to John what you hear and see: The blind receive sight, the lame walk, those who have leprosy are cured, the deaf hear, the dead are raised, and the good news is preached to the poor" (Matthew 11:4, 5).

Attention Grabber

On a poster board or a computer, make a simple "Good Newspaper." Help the kids write headlines telling about Jesus based on this verse, and then let them draw pictures to illustrate.

Living It

John the Baptist's disciples wanted to know if Jesus was the Messiah. Jesus answered by describing his miracles and preaching. This verse tells a lot about Jesus' ministry. Other verses tell us what the good news is that is preached to the poor. The good news is that Jesus is the Christ (Acts 5:42); that there is peace through Jesus Christ, who is Lord of all (Acts 10:36); that Jesus rose from the dead (Acts 13:37); and that there is forgiveness of sins through Jesus (Acts 13:38, 39). Many people have heard the gospel shared as if it were bad news, because it was told reluctantly, apologetically, or negatively. How can we share it as good news? With enthusiasm and joy!

Discussion Questions

◉ What does the word "gospel" mean? (good news)
◉ How do the things Jesus did that are described in this verse show he is God's Son?

Prayer Prompter

Thank you for the good news! Please help us to spread it.

Actions Show Wisdom
Matthew 11:16-19

Memory Verse
"But wisdom is proved right by her actions" (Matthew 11:19).

Attention Grabber
Ask everyone about nicknames they have had.

Living It
As you know, people are called bad names as well as good ones. When that happens to you, don't feel too bad. Jesus was perfect and yet people called him bad names. They didn't want to agree with him, because they didn't like what he was saying. When Jesus said, "But wisdom is proved right by her actions," he was saying that the wisdom of his message would come through in what he did. Don't be discouraged if people put you down for being a Christian; if we continue to follow Jesus, our lives will show the wisdom of his message.

Discussion Question
⊙ Your life may not be very different from other kids' lives right now, but how will the wisdom of Jesus' message show in your life when you are a teen? (While other teens are drinking, taking drugs, and having promiscuous relationships, the teens who follow Jesus are spared the consequences of those behaviors.)

Prayer Prompter
When others look at our lives, please help them to see that it is wise to follow you.

Shown to Children
Matthew 11:25

Memory Verse
At that time Jesus said, "I praise you, Father, Lord of heaven and earth, because you have hidden these things from the wise and learned, and revealed them to little children" (Matthew 11:25).

Attention Grabber
Beforehand, write or print out from the computer a simple "diploma" for each child that says "_____ (name) is smart to believe and follow Jesus" and roll it into a scroll. Show the kids an actual diploma and tassel if you have them. Then present them with the diplomas you made and let them drip a candle's wax at the bottom of the diploma for a seal or cut a seal from aluminum foil to glue onto the bottom of the diploma.

Living It
Many people spend most of their lives getting educated and yet miss learning what is most important to know: that Jesus wants to be their Savior and Lord. The Bible warns that in the last days people will be "always learning but never able to acknowledge the truth" (2 Timothy 3:7).

Discussion Question
◎ Why does God sometimes reveal himself more to little children than adults?

Prayer Prompter
Please help us continue to believe and follow you.

I Will Give You Rest
Matthew 11:28

Memory Verse
"Come to me, all you who are weary and burdened, and I will give you rest" (Matthew 11:28).

Attention Grabber
Make a large pile of small objects on a dinner plate. Objects representing responsibilities, such as a textbook for homework or a sponge for chores, are especially good. Ask what it means to "have too much on our plate." (We feel we have too much to do.)

Living It
When we try to do too much or we try to handle our problems and responsibilities without Jesus, we can feel exhausted and overwhelmed, as if we're carrying a heavy load. When we turn our cares over to Jesus, he makes us feel better. He helps us accomplish things we couldn't do on our own. He says, "My grace is sufficient for you, for my power is made perfect in weakness" (2 Corinthians 12:9). Some people are weary and burdened from trying to do enough good deeds to deserve heaven, which is impossible. It is a great relief for people to come to Jesus and find that it's God's grace instead of their own good works that gets them into heaven. Then they serve out of love for God.

Discussion Questions
- Are you trying to be "good enough"?
- How can Jesus help?

Prayer Prompter
Please remind us to come to you. Help us not to feel weary and burdened.

Take My Yoke Upon You

Matthew 11:29

Memory Verse

"Take my yoke upon you and learn from me, for I am gentle and humble in heart, and you will find rest for your souls" (Matthew 11:29).

Attention Grabber

Place a picture of Jesus (an illustration from a Bible storybook) in front of the kids. Have them write words that describe Jesus on small pieces of paper and then attach them around the picture.

Living It

Some people don't come to Jesus because they're afraid that he is mad at them, that he will punish them, and he will give them too much to do. Actually, he is gentle and forgiving. He helps our souls feel peaceful, not overworked. The more we get to know him, the more we love him!

Discussion Question

- Why do we need a yoke? (A yoke is a symbol of being obedient to God and letting him direct our work, which helps us and those whom we serve.)

Prayer Prompter

Remind us not to try to carry our burdens and responsibilities alone without you. Help us to see you as you truly are—gentle and humble. Help us let our souls rest in you rather than being troubled and burdened.

My Burden Is Light
Matthew 11:30

Memory Verse

"For my yoke is easy and my burden is light" (Matthew 11:30).

Attention Grabber

Connect two yolks from boiled eggs with a toothpick to form "barbells." Announce that you are a weight lifter and lift the "barbells." Tell the kids your yolk is easy and your burden is light. When they stop groaning, ask them to describe the yoke to which Jesus referred.

Living It

If we listen to God in our prayers, he will tell us what he wants to do with our lives. What he asks of us will never be too hard or burdensome for us if we trust him to help us. He promises us in 2 Corinthians 9:8 that he "is able to make all grace abound to you, so that in all things at all times, having all that you need, you will abound in every good work." Whenever you start to feel overwhelmed as you serve God, recite Philippians 4:13 to yourself. It says, "I can do everything through him who gives me strength." God will "not forget your work and the love you have shown him as you have helped his people and continue to help them" (Hebrews 6:10).

Discussion Question

◉ Why is Jesus' burden light? (Because he helps us carry it, he gives us what we need, and he strengthens us.)

Prayer Prompter

Please help us trust you so that your yoke and burden will be light for us.

Do Good on the Sabbath

Matthew 12:11, 12

Memory Verse

He said to them, "If any of you has a sheep and it falls into a pit on the Sabbath, will you not take hold of it and lift it out? How much more valuable is a man than a sheep! Therefore it is lawful to do good on the Sabbath" (Matthew 12:11, 12).

Attention Grabber

Plan some good things you can do for others this Sunday. Give the kids a list of things to choose from, such as write letters to missionaries, visit the elderly, or call family members who live far away. Consider having them write an acrostic poem in which each line starts with a letter from the word S-U-N-D-A-Y.

Living It

In Bible times, some people had gotten so fanatical that they wouldn't even tie knots on the Sabbath because they considered it "work." Jesus said that we can do good every day of the week. Sunday is an especially good day to serve others! We can use our free time to be with our family and help other people together.

Discussion Question

◉ How are our Sundays different from the other days of the week?

Prayer Prompter

Please help us to get rested and help others on our Sundays.

Do Good on the Sabbath

Memory Verse

Jesus knew their thoughts and said to them, "Every kingdom divided against itself will be ruined, and every city or household divided against itself will not stand" (Matthew 12:25).

Attention Grabber

Have the kids do an impersonation of a dog chasing its tail. Point out that it's hard for anything that is fighting itself to keep from falling down.

Living It

Jesus said these words when he was accused of being the prince of demons after he cast a demon out of someone. He was saying that Satan wouldn't fight against his own evil kingdom, so Jesus was obviously from the kingdom of God instead.

Discussion Questions

◉ What does it mean to be united?
◉ How can our family be more united?

Prayer Prompter

Please help us recognize evil around us so we can resist it.

Who Is on the Lord's Side?
Matthew 12:30

Memory Verse
"He who is not with me is against me, and he who does not gather with me scatters" (Matthew 12:30).

Attention Grabber
Divide the family into two teams for a game, letting the kids choose which team to join. Then have a simple relay race. Emphasize that no one could stand in the sidelines—everyone had to be on one side or the other.

Living It
Joshua said "Choose for yourselves this day whom you will serve... But as for me and my household, we will serve the Lord" (Joshua 24:15). Everyone has to make that decision. God doesn't like it when people don't commit to him; he says, "I know your deeds, that you are neither cold nor hot. I wish you were either one or the other! So, because you are lukewarm—neither hot nor cold—I am about to spit you out of my mouth" (Revelation 3:15, 16).

Discussion Question
◎ Which of your actions show that you are committed to Jesus?

Prayer Prompter
Please help us to be committed to you and to show it by how we live.

Every Careless Word

Memory Verse

"But I tell you that men will have to give account on the day of judgment for every careless word they have spoken" (Matthew 12:36).

Attention Grabber

Have each person tell a joke or fairy-tale plot without using the words "a," "an," "the," or "was." Emphasize that they had to choose their words very carefully.

Living It

It's difficult to think about our words before we speak them. But if we don't, they can cause a great deal of damage that is sometimes impossible to undo. Name-calling can hurt relationships and the other person's self-respect. Gossip can cause the listeners to reject and judge others. James 3:5, 6 says, "Consider what a great forest is set on fire by a small spark. The tongue also is a fire, a world of evil among the parts of the body. It corrupts the whole person, sets the whole course of his life on fire, and is itself set on fire by hell."

Discussion Questions

- In what situations in your daily life is it especially easy to gossip?
- Why should we be careful of what we say?

Prayer Prompter

Please help us to be careful of what we say.

Three Days
Matthew 12:39, 40

Memory Verse
"For as Jonah was three days and three nights in the belly of a huge fish, so the Son of Man will be three days and three nights in the heart of the earth" (Matthew 12:40).

Attention Grabber
Serve tuna or sardines and remind the kids that this is how the inside of the fish might have smelled to Jonah. Let them mold aluminum foil into a fish and make a small Jonah to fit inside.

Living It
It wasn't a coincidence that Jonah was in the giant fish for three days; that's how long Jesus would be in the tomb. Many Old Testament verses mention things that later happened to Jesus. This is called foreshadowing or prophecy.

Discussion Question
⊙ Do you need to see a sign to know that Jesus is God's Son? Why or why not?

Prayer Prompter
Thank you for all the ways that Bible stories help us understand who you are. Please help us to have faith in you, whether we see miraculous signs or not.

Be Good Soil
Matthew 13:1-9, 18-23

Memory Verse

"But the one who received the seed that fell on good soil is the man who hears the word and understands it. He produces a crop, yielding a hundred, sixty or thirty times what was sown" (Matthew 13:23).

Attention Grabber

Plant seeds in a cup filled with potting soil. Use kernels of unpopped popcorn or seeds from a piece of fruit or a vegetable if necessary. Emphasize that God wants our hearts to be like the good soil in which the message of his kingdom grows and eventually produces fruit—"love, joy, peace, patience, kindness, goodness, faithfulness, gentleness, and self control" (Galatians 5:22).

Living It

Let's make a simple chart. (Draw a three-column chart with the following headings. Let your family fill in what is italicized.)

Landing spot	Result for seed	Result for people
path	*birds ate*	*Don't understand and evil one snatches them*
rocks	*dried up*	*Trouble or persecution causes them to fall away*
thorns	*choked*	*Worries of life and deceitfulness of wealth choke their faith*
good soil	*produced fruit*	*Produce even more faith than what was sown into their own lives*

Discussion Question

◉ Look at the third column. How can we keep our faith growing healthy and strong?

Prayer Prompter

Please grow your truth in our hearts. Help us stay away from what could harm our faith.

Wheat and Weeds

Matthew 13:24-30, 36-43

Memory Verse

Jesus told them another parable: "The kingdom of heaven is like a man who sowed good seed in his field. But while everyone was sleeping, his enemy came and sowed weeds among the wheat, and went away" (Matthew 13:24, 25).

Attention Grabber

Have a weed-pulling contest. Who can pull the most in two minutes? (Only weeds with roots count!) If you have any wheat in a flower arrangement or pictured in art in your home, show it to the kids and tell them that wheat is ground to make flour. Read the whole parable aloud. Explain that the wheat represents people who believe in Jesus; the weeds represent people who do not.

Living It

Believers and non-believers all live together in the world now. But at the end of the world, Jesus will separate those who believe (the wheat) from those who don't believe (the weeds). Those who believe will live in heaven forever with Jesus. Those who don't will be separated from him forever. While we live here among people who don't believe, we need to share the good news about Jesus with them.

Discussion Question

◉ What are the hardest things about being wheat (Christians) among weeds (non-believers)?

Prayer Prompter

Thank you for your promise that we can live in heaven with you forever.

Memory Verse

He told them another parable: "The kingdom of heaven is like a mustard seed, which a man took and planted in his field. Though it is the smallest of all your seeds, yet when it grows, it is the largest of garden plants and becomes a tree, so that the birds of the air come and perch in its branches" (Matthew 13:31, 32).

Attention Grabber

Serve pretzels with mustard for dipping. Explain that mustard is made from ground-up mustard seeds. If you have mustard seeds, show the kids how small they are.

Living It

God's kingdom started small, but it has grown tremendously. When Jesus was on the earth, the number of believers could fit on a hillside. Now there are millions and millions. Eventually his gospel will reach every country (Revelation 14:6). Don't be discouraged if you're not surrounded by believers—they're out there and their number is growing!

Discussion Question

◉ How do you feel strengthened when you are around other believers?

Prayer Prompter

Please use us to help your kingdom grow.

Yeast in the Dough
Matthew 13:33

Memory Verse
He told them still another parable: "The kingdom of heaven is like yeast that a woman took and mixed into a large amount of flour until it worked all through the dough" (Matthew 13:33).

Attention Grabber
If you have yeast available, let the kids smell it. If you have a bread machine, let the kids pour in the ingredients. (You might want to make something special such as raisin bread.) Explain that yeast spreads quickly throughout the dough, making it light and fluffy. Otherwise the bread would be flat.

Living It
Yeast is actually alive. When a baker combines it with the other ingredients of a loaf of bread, the yeast quickly grows and spreads throughout the dough, making the dough rise. You can be like yeast, too. When you really understand and accept how much God loves you, you want to share what Jesus has done for you with others. It feels great to have the weight of your guilt lifted. You have peace because you know that you are deeply loved. You love God in return and want to obey him to show it. Those positive changes are noticeable to others, and people want to find out what is making the difference. Just like yeast, you can make a difference all around you!

Discussion Question
◎ How can you help spread the good news through the world?

Prayer Prompter
Help us have a sincere, life-changing relationship with you that spreads to others like yeast through dough.

A Pearl of Great Price

Matthew 13:45, 46

Memory Verse

"Again, the kingdom of heaven is like a merchant looking for fine pearls. When he found one of great value, he went away and sold everything he had and bought it" (Matthew 13:45, 46).

Attention Grabber

Play the shell game with three shells and a faux or real pearl. Or play it with three cups and a ball. Place the pearl or ball under one of the shells or cups. Move the shells or cups around, and let the kids guess where the pearl or ball is now.

Living It

Just as you searched for the pearl, people spend their whole lives searching for what will make them happy. When they finally find Jesus, they are so thrilled that they are willing to give up whatever it takes to follow him.

Discussion Questions

◉ How has coming into the Kingdom of God been valuable to you?

◉ Why has it been worth anything you gave up for it?

Prayer Prompter

Thank you for giving us the valuable truth about Jesus. We love you! Help us tell others about the way to be deeply happy.

Like a Net
Matthew 13:47-50

Memory Verse
"Once again, the kingdom of heaven is like a net that was let down into the lake and caught all kinds of fish" (Matthew 13:47).

Attention Grabber
Mix two flavors of goldfish-shaped crackers in a bowl. Draw fishing nets on two plates. Have the kids separate the fish onto the two different plates.

Living It
The parable Jesus told in today's reading says that there are good fish and bad fish in God's kingdom right now, but someday the angels will sort the wicked from the righteous. The only way to be righteous (right with God) is through trusting Jesus to take away your sins and showing that faith by following him. "Righteousness from God comes through faith in Jesus Christ to all who believe" (Romans 3:22). First John 3:6, 7 says, "No one who lives in him keeps on sinning. No one who continues to sin has either seen him or known him. Dear children, do not let anyone lead you astray. He who does what is right is righteous, just as he is righteous."

Discussion Questions
◉ What does it mean to be righteous?
◉ Are you righteous in God's sight? Why or why not?

Prayer Prompter
Please give us faith in Jesus that makes us right with you, and help us to live in a way that reflects that faith.

Old and New Treasures

Memory Verse

He said to them, "Therefore every teacher of the law who has been instructed about the kingdom of heaven is like the owner of a house who brings out of his storeroom new treasures as well as old" (Matthew 13:52).

Attention Grabber

Share your favorite Old Testament verse and your favorite New Testament verse with the kids. Explain how those verses have helped you in your life.

Living It

Teachers who have the Old Testament and the New Testament to share are rich. They have plenty of valuable lessons to teach. Remember that the Bible says, "All Scripture is God-breathed and is useful for teaching, rebuking, correcting and training in righteousness" (2 Timothy 3:16).

Discussion Questions

◎ How are our devotions helping you?
◎ What would help you to remember the verses better?

Prayer Prompter

Thank you for your holy Word, Lord. Please help us show how much we treasure it by studying it and applying your teachings that are in it.

No Hometown Honor
Matthew 13:53-58; Mark 6:4

Memory Verse
And they took offense at him. But Jesus said to them, "Only in his hometown and in his own house is a prophet without honor" *(Matthew 13:57).*

Attention Grabber
Write negative words such as "loser," "dummy," and "failure" on adhesive labels. Stick the labels on your clothes. Explain that sometimes other people who think they know us well don't see our potential; they put negative labels on us. But we don't have to let those labels stick (remove the labels). And we need to make sure we don't do that to others.

Living It
It's amazing that many of the people in Jesus' hometown, and even in his own family, couldn't see that he was the Son of God. They just saw him as a carpenter's son and the relative of people they knew. He didn't do many miracles there because of their lack of faith. Although no one has a mission as great as Jesus', God has a plan for every person. Don't be discouraged from following God even when others don't seem to have confidence in you.

Discussion Questions
- If you knew God's plan for your family members and people at school, how would you treat them better?
- Who has confidence in you and believes that you will try to follow God's plan for your life?

Prayer Prompter
Please help us to see the best in others and treat them with respect. Help us to have confidence that you will be able to use us even if others don't always see our potential.

For the Sake of Tradition

Memory Verse
Jesus replied, "And why do you break the command of God for the sake of your tradition?" (Matthew 15:3).

Attention Grabber
Give each child a sandwich bag. For each of the Ten Commandments they can remember (from Exodus 20), give them a "commandmint." Use a peppermint swirl candy, butter mint, or homemade mints (see page 266). When everyone has tried, write down the Ten Commandments. Ask how our society encourages or discourages us from keeping them.

Living It
There are both good and bad traditions. Holidays can be good traditions that remind us of important events, bring our family closer together, and help us focus on God. Bad traditions are customs we follow to please other people even though they go against what God wants. For example, since it's uncommon for people to talk about Jesus in everyday conversations, some of us let that tradition keep us from sharing the truth about him. Unfortunately, that is only one example of many. Paul asked a question that is good for us to ask ourselves, "Am I now trying to win the approval of men, or of God? Or am I trying to please men? If I were still trying to please men, I would not be a servant of Christ" (Galatians 1:10).

Discussion Question
◉ In what ways are you willing to break traditions and customs to obey God?

Prayer Prompter
Please help us to obey you even when it doesn't match our traditions.

Help Your Parents

Matthew 15:5, 6; Mark 7:9-13

Memory Verse

"But you say that if a man says to his father or mother, 'Whatever help you might otherwise have received from me is a gift devoted to God,' he is not to 'honor his father' with it. Thus you nullify the word of God for the sake of your tradition" (Matthew 15:5, 6).

Attention Grabber

Call your children's grandparents on the phone together, or make a homemade card for the grandparents and write notes in it.

Living It

Our country has laws that say parents must be responsible for their children. Our laws don't force children to take responsibility for helping their parents. But God says we need to do that as part of obeying his command to honor your father and mother.

Discussion Questions

- How can I help my parents (your grandparents) more?
- How can you help your parents more?

Prayer Prompter

Please help the members of our family to take good care of each other.

Unclean Words
Matthew 15:11, 17-20; Mark 7:14-23

Memory Verse

"What goes into a man's mouth does not make him 'unclean,' but what comes out of his mouth, that is what makes him 'unclean'" *(Matthew 15:11).*

Attention Grabber

Ask, "Have you ever heard of kids getting their mouths washed out with soap if they say dirty words?" Have your kids write the verse with permanent marker on a bar of soap or a bottle of liquid soap. Or pretend to eat dirt (crushed Oreo sandwich cookies or crushed graham crackers) from a terra-cotta pot lined with plastic food wrap. Ask the kids if it's true that you are what you eat and that you are dirty if you eat dirt. Explain to them that what you eat doesn't make you dirty, but if you say dirty things, you need for God to cleanse you. Let the children have the crumbs sprinkled over instant pudding.

Living It

Some religions have strict rules about what people can and cannot eat and drink. Jesus said it's not what goes into our mouths that's sinful; it's what comes out of them (what we say) that is actually what's sinful.

Discussion Question

◎ If your conversations had been recorded all day yesterday, would you mind if the tape were played for our family? Why or why not?

Prayer Prompter

Please purify our hearts so what comes out of our mouths will be pure.

Blind Guides
Matthew 15:14

Memory Verse
"Leave them; they are blind guides. If a blind man leads a blind man, both will fall into a pit" (Matthew 15:14).

Attention Grabber
Blindfold the kids and have them try to lead each other. Watch them carefully so they don't get hurt.

Living It
We are being influenced and led every day, sometimes when we're unaware. Most people think advertising doesn't influence them, but companies pay millions for commercials because they know people are influenced by them. Let's take turns saying part of a slogan or jingle and see if the rest of us can finish it. Jesus said it's important to be careful who you are following. Make sure those who lead you can see that Jesus is the way to the Father.

Discussion Questions
◉ Who leads you?
◉ Why do they lead you?

Prayer Prompter
Please help us to be sure we're following people who are following you.

Jesus Has Compassion
Matthew 15:32-38; Mark 8:1-10

Memory Verse
Jesus called his disciples to him and said, "I have compassion for these people; they have already been with me three days and have nothing to eat. I do not want to send them away hungry, or they may collapse on the way" (Matthew 15:32).

Attention Grabber
Give each person oyster crackers (representing miniature round loaves of bread) and goldfish-shaped crackers. For fun, hold a plate under the end of a table and let your kids compete to see who can flick their crackers closest to the end of the table without going off onto the plate. If you would prefer, make a meal of tuna and bread instead.

Living It
Jesus taught people for three days straight without stopping for food! He felt compassion for the people and didn't want them to faint from hunger on their way home, so he miraculously fed a crowd of at least four thousand with only seven loaves of bread and a few small fish. Jesus has compassion for you, too.

Discussion Question
◉ Do you feel that Jesus has compassion for you in the situations you face right now? Why or why not?

Prayer Prompter
Thank you for the compassion you feel for us and show to us. Help us to believe the truth that you care about everything in our lives.

The Signs of the Times
Matthew 16:2, 3

Memory Verse
"You know how to interpret the appearance of the sky, but you cannot interpret the signs of the times" (Matthew 16:3).

Attention Grabber
Look at the sky together and discuss whether it looks as if it will rain. If desired, make a seven-day chart in which the kids can illustrate the weather.

Living It
Jesus emphasized that we know a lot about things that matter a little (the weather) and only a little about what matters very much (what the Bible says will happen). In Jesus' time, some people didn't know the signs of the times enough to realize that the Son of God had come to earth. We need to make sure that we know Jesus and that we try to understand what the Bible says will happen.

Discussion Questions
◉ What do you think about most during the day?
◉ Can you name two events the Bible says will happen before Jesus returns?

Prayer Prompter
Please help us to know what the Bible says will happen and to recognize when it is happening. Make the things that are important to you important to us, too.

You Are the Christ
Matthew 16:15-17; Mark 8:29

Memory Verse
"But what about you?" he asked. "Who do you say I am?" Simon Peter answered, "You are the Christ, the Son of the living God" (Matthew 16:15, 16).

Attention Grabber
Sing "I Am a C-H-R-I-S-T-I-A-N" if you know it. Explain that some people think they're Christians just because they go to church. Tell the kids the Bible says it's important to meet together (Hebrews 10:25), but that isn't what makes us Christians. Ask if they've heard the saying that church is not what makes you a Christian any more than standing in a garage makes you a car. Have them continue with similar analogies (for example, any more than sitting in a garden makes you a rutabaga, or any more than swimming in an aquarium makes you a guppy).

Living It
Christians are people who trust Jesus as Savior and Lord. When you ask Jesus to be your Savior, it means you want him to save you from punishment for your sins because you believe he took that punishment for you on the cross. When you ask him to be your Lord, it means you want to follow him as your leader.

Discussion Question
◉ What would you like to know about becoming a Christian? (If you sense your child is interested in accepting Jesus as Savior and Lord, you may wish to turn to page 268 for help.)

Prayer Prompter
Thank you for sending your Son, the Christ, as you promised you would. Please help everyone in our entire family to become Christians.

Take Up Your Cross

Matthew 16:24; Mark 8:34

Memory Verse

Then Jesus said to his disciples, "If anyone would come after me, he must deny himself and take up his cross and follow me" (Matthew 16:24).

Attention Grabber

Gather twigs together to make crosses. Let the kids place one stick on top of another and wrap the section where they cross with yarn, twine, thread, or embroidery floss. Use pushpins to hang one in each family member's bedroom. Ask, "What does the cross remind us of?" (Jesus died on a cross to take the punishment for our sins so we could go to heaven.)

Living It

In Jesus' time, people had to watch others carry crosses on which they would be crucified. Jesus' followers saw this happen many times. When he told them that following him meant taking up their cross, he may have meant two things. One is that they had to be willing to risk their lives, and the other is that they had to be born again, letting their old sinful nature die (be crucified). In Galatians 2:20 Paul said it this way: "I have been crucified with Christ and I no longer live, but Christ lives in me."

Discussion Questions

- What selfish desires have you left behind to follow Jesus?
- What is still a struggle for you?
- Why is giving up selfish desires worthwhile?

Prayer Prompter

Thank you for the privilege of living in a country in which we can worship you without fearing death. Please help us to be committed enough that we would worship you even if we didn't have that freedom. Please help us daily to recommit to you and nail our selfishness to the cross.

Take Up Your Cross

Lose Life and Find It
Matthew 16:25; Mark 8:35; John 12:25

Memory Verse
"For whoever wants to save his life will lose it, but whoever loses his life for me will find it" (Matthew 16:25).

Attention Grabber
Beforehand, cut a big tag out of posterboard for each family member. Punch a hole in each, thread a piece of twine or yarn through it, and knot it. Write "For God" on yours, and hang it around your neck. Ask each family member to think about whether his life belongs to him or whether he has given it to God. Have them choose to write "Mine, Mine, All Mine" or "For God" on one side of their tag and the memory verse on the other side. They can wear the tags during the devotion and then later hang them in their rooms to help them remember the verse.

Living It
Keeping your life means making your decisions based on selfish desires. People who save their lives for themselves lose out on the joy and rewards of following Jesus. To lose our lives for Jesus' sake means to give him our lives to use however he wants. When we do this, we have more rewarding lives here and we will live forever with God. Romans 8:13, 14 says, "For if you live according to the sinful nature, you will die; but if by the Spirit you put to death the misdeeds of the body, you will live, because those who are led by the Spirit of God are sons of God."

Discussion Questions
- Do you spend each day just doing whatever you feel like doing, or do you let God lead you through the Holy Spirit?
- How could God use you to help others in the career you think you might want to do?

Prayer Prompter
Please use our lives however you want. Help us to listen for the Holy Spirit leading us.

Don't Trade Your Soul
Matthew 16:26; Mark 8:36

Memory Verse
"What good will it be for a man if he gains the whole world, yet forfeits his soul? Or what can a man give in exchange for his soul?" (Matthew 16:26).

Attention Grabber
Write "money," "approval," "fame," "power," and "possessions" on very small scraps of paper. Explain that many people are like vacuum cleaners, going through life trying to suck up things that seem tremendously valuable. (Use a mini vacuum cleaner to suck up the scraps.) But when their lives are over, they are full of junk inside (open the mini vacuum cleaner and show the contents). Trading our lives for these things is not a good deal.

Living It
The world will tell you to spend all of your time and energy getting money, belongings, and pleasure. It doesn't matter if you gain everything there is if you lose your soul. That can happen if we spend so much time and energy on those things that we never get to know God, or if we get those things by being heartless toward people (climbing over them to get to the top or ignoring needs that we could help).

Discussion Question
◉ What is the difference between the world's definition of "having it all" and the believers'?

Prayer Prompter
Please help us not to give our life to things that don't really matter.

Don't Trade Your Soul

Memory Verse

"For the Son of Man is going to come in his Father's glory with his angels, and then he will reward each person according to what he has done" (Matthew 16:27).

Attention Grabber

Have the kids gather leaves and staple them together to make a crown. Have silly races (crab walk, human wheelbarrow, hopping, etc.) and let the winner of each race wear the crown until the next winner gets to wear it.

Living It

Explain that in Bible times, winning athletes wore crowns made of laurel leaves. Paul said, "Everyone who competes in the games goes into strict training. They do it to get a crown that will not last; but we do it to get a crown that will last forever" (1 Corinthians 9:25). James 1:12 says, "Blessed is the man who perseveres under trial, because when he has stood the test, he will receive the crown of life that God has promised to those who love him." A crown of life is one of the rewards God will give us for following Jesus.

Discussion Questions

- In what ways does God already reward you here on earth?
- How will you feel if people in heaven thank you for telling them about Jesus?
- Who would you especially want to see?

Prayer Prompter

Please help us to live in a way that pleases you.

Mustard Seed Faith
Matthew 17:18-21; Luke 17:6

Memory Verse
"I tell you the truth, if you have faith as small as a mustard seed, you can say to this mountain, 'Move from here to there' and it will move. Nothing will be impossible for you" (Matthew 17:20, 21).

Attention Grabber
Have the kids write their problems on paper cups and stack them like a mountain. Say, "This is faith." Hand them a small ball to throw at the mountain of cups. When they knock down the cups, tell them that faith in God is just as powerful to knock down our mountains of problems.

Living It
Sometimes we don't actively trust God to help us with our problems. Jesus said that if we have faith the size of a tiny mustard seed, God will do things that would be impossible for us to do. Trusting God to help us can solve even the largest problems.

Discussion Question
◎ What problems do you have right now that you can trust God to take care of?

Prayer Prompter
Please give us the faith to trust that you will help us when we ask.

Mustard Seed Faith

Like Little Children
Matthew 18:3

Memory Verse
And he said: "I tell you the truth, unless you change and become like little children, you will never enter the kingdom of heaven" (Matthew 18:3).

Attention Grabber
Have baby races—crawling races and racing to feed each other baby food (cottage cheese, applesauce, or pudding). Explain that we need to outgrow some childish behaviors, but there are child-like behaviors and attitudes that are good to keep. Look at your children's baby pictures, and talk about the sweet qualities they had as babies and young children.

Living It
As you are growing into adults, there are some qualities that Jesus doesn't want you to leave behind. Some of the child-like qualities people need to come into God's kingdom are being loving, humble, teachable, and trusting toward God.

Discussion Question
◎ What is the difference between childish and child-like?

Prayer Prompter
Please help us be loving, humble, teachable, and trusting.

The Humble Are Greatest
Matthew 18:4

Memory Verse
"Therefore, whoever humbles himself like this child is the greatest in the kingdom of heaven" (Matthew 18:4).

Attention Grabber
Let the kids switch roles with you during a meal or for an hour. If they are young enough to enjoy it, let them dress up in your clothes and play "Mother, May I?" but instead call it "Father, May I?" to remind them to be humble and obedient before their Father in heaven.

Living It
It may seem as if adults get to do whatever they want. Actually, God wants adults to be like children who do what their father tells them. It's just that instead of obeying our earthly fathers, we are obeying our heavenly Father. Jesus said we shouldn't act proud and as if we don't need God; he wants us to humble ourselves like children.

Discussion Question
◎ How can we be more humble and respectful to God in our prayers? In our speech? In how we listen for the Holy Spirit? In other ways?

Prayer Prompter
Please help us to be more humble and respectful to you.

Welcome Children
Matthew 18:5; Mark 9:36, 37; Luke 9:48

Memory Verse
"And whoever welcomes a child like this in my name welcomes me"
(Matthew 18:5).

Attention Grabber
Make plans for each of the kids to invite a friend to spend the night on a Saturday night (all on one night or on subsequent Saturday nights), and then attend church with your family the following morning. Make plans for snacks, games, and ways you can tell the friends about Jesus before, during, or after church.

Living It
A large percentage of people who accept Jesus as their Savior will do so while they are children. When kids are young, they are more open to hearing the truth about Jesus. It's important to share with them while they are willing to learn. One of the ways to share with them is to tell them why you became a Christian and then ask them if they would like to do that too. Another way is to bring them with us to church and to try to find a time before, after, or during the lesson when we can talk about everyone's need for Jesus to be his or her own personal Savior and Lord. (For more information, see page 268.)

Discussion Question
◉ When new people (kids or adults) come to church, how can we make them feel welcome?

Prayer Prompter
Please help us welcome other children into your kingdom.

Don't Cause Sin
Matthew 18:6; Mark 9:32; Luke 17:2

Memory Verse

"But if anyone causes one of these little ones who believe in me to sin, it would be better for him to have a large millstone hung around his neck and to be drowned in the depths of the sea" (Matthew 18:6).

Attention Grabber

Let the kids take turns rubbing two flat rocks together to grind sunflower seeds (or other seeds). Explain that millstones were big rocks that people used to grind wheat into flour. The rocks were rubbed together with wheat kernels between them. They were heavy and they sank very quickly if dropped in water.

Living It

God loves you and other children very, very much. He holds grown-ups responsible for how they treat you. If someone tried to get you to do something wrong, God wouldn't take that lightly. He wants everyone to teach children the truth and to encourage them to do what's right.

Discussion Question

◉ How can we encourage others to do what's right without nagging them or making them feel judged?

Prayer Prompter

Please keep children safe from evil. Help us to be careful to make sure we teach what's true and that we have a good influence on others.

These Little Ones
Matthew 18:10

Memory Verse

"See that you do not look down on one of these little ones. For I tell you that their angels in heaven always see the face of my Father in heaven" (Matthew 18:10).

Attention Grabber

If you have angel decorations in your home, see if the kids can close their eyes and remember them. Do the kids remember making snow angels by lying on a snowdrift and waving their arms and legs? Show them how to fold a piece of paper accordion-style and cut out a chain of angels. (See the pattern on page ??.) If you have a tube of sugar cookie dough or time to make your own, cut and bake angel-shaped cookies. Use a ball of dough for the head, a triangle for the body, and a half-circle for each wing.

Living It

God wants everyone to treat children with respect and to understand how important you are. Jesus said you even have angels who see God all day and night! Let's look up angels in our concordance and find verses about them in the Bible so we can find out what they do and what they look like.

Discussion Questions

- ◉ How can adults treat you to show that they respect you?
- ◉ How can you show respect to younger children?

Prayer Prompter

Please help all of us to treat children with respect.

A Lost Sheep
Matthew 18:12-14

Memory Verse

"What do you think? If a man owns a hundred sheep, and one of them wanders away, will he not leave the ninety-nine on the hills and go to look for the one that wandered off?" (Matthew 18:12).

Attention Grabber

Tell the kids to hide and baa like a sheep until you find them. When you locate each of them, act overjoyed and carry them back on your shoulders or back (if they're not so big that they'll give you a hernia!). Emphasize how happy the shepherd was to find his sheep and how he didn't give up.

Living It

God loves you so much! Even when you wander away from him, he doesn't stop loving you. He will search for you and carry you back. If you are ever lost in sin, call out to him. He will hear you and help you.

Discussion Question

◉ Who tries to convince us that God doesn't want us when we have sinned? (the devil)

Prayer Prompter

Thank you for loving us. Please keep us close to you, Lord. If we ever wander away from you, please bring us back quickly.

A Lost Sheep

Between the Two of You
Matthew 18:15-17

Memory Verse
"If your brother sins against you, go and show him his fault, just between the two of you. If he listens to you, you have won your brother over" (Matthew 18:15).

Attention Grabber
Attach a large safety pin to the belt of a robe. Ask, "If this were our family's 'tattle tail,' would you want to wear it? Why not?"

Living It
When someone does something wrong to us, God doesn't want us to gossip or tattle. If a problem between you and another child is big enough that you can't just overlook it, he wants you to try to work it out with that person. Only if that person won't listen, should you get other people to help you work it out. However, if you are scared or uncomfortable, or if your problem is with an adult, you should always tell your parents.

Discussion Questions
- If someone thinks you have done something wrong, would you prefer that he talk to you directly? Why?
- There are many different ways someone could tell you that you did something wrong to them. Which would make you mad? Which would cause you to make excuses? Which would make you want to ask the person's forgiveness and change your behavior?

Prayer Prompter
Please help us learn to work out our problems with people directly.

When Two Agree in Prayer

Matthew 18:19

Memory Verse

"Again, I tell you that if two of you on earth agree about anything you ask for, it will be done for you by my Father in heaven" (Matthew 18:19).

Attention Grabber

Make a handkerchief, piece of fabric, or tube sock into a Lone Ranger's mask by cutting two eyeholes out of it. Let at least one of the kids wear the mask and ride on your back as if you're a horse. Have everyone hum the Lone Ranger's theme (the "William Tell Overture," by Giocchino Rossini).

Living It

God doesn't want us to be Lone Rangers when it comes to praying. What was Queen Esther's problem and what did she do? (The king planned to kill all of the Jews, which meant she would die, too. She asked all of the Jews to fast and pray with her. See Esther 3:8–4:16.) When we face problems, it's good to ask others to pray with us. And it's good to offer to pray for others who need God's help. James 5:16 says, "Confess your sins to each other and pray for each other so that you may be healed. The prayer of a righteous man is powerful and effective."

Discussion Questions

◉ What keeps us from asking other people to pray for us?
◉ How do you feel when other people pray for you?

Prayer Prompter

(Be especially sure to ask for the family's prayer requests today!) Please help us to tell others when we need for them to pray for us. Please help us not to be too shy to offer to pray for people.

Two or Three Together
Matthew 18:20

Memory Verse

"For where two or three come together in my name, there am I with them" (Matthew 18:20).

Attention Grabber

Ask the kids what it means to come together in Jesus' name (because of him, for him, to worship him, or to learn about him). Ask, "Does this verse apply to our family gathering for devotions?" (Yes.) "How could you feel if you could actually see him?" Mention that angels and Jesus often said, "Do not be afraid" when they appeared to people in the Bible, and that people, though shocked at first, usually rejoiced afterward.

Living It

It's comforting to know that when we gather together to talk about Jesus or worship him, he is really right here with us. How can we honor him at that time by what we say and how we behave?

Discussion Question

◉ Do you feel Jesus' presence while worshiping him at church?

Prayer Prompter

Thank you for being with us when we gather together to talk about you and worship you. Please help us to give you glory at those times and always.

Forgive and Forgive

Matthew 18:21, 22; Luke 17:3-6

Memory Verse

Then Peter came to Jesus and asked, "Lord, how many times shall I forgive my brother when he sins against me? Up to seven times?" Jesus answered, "I tell you, not seven times, but seventy-seven times" (Matthew 18:21, 22).

Attention Grabber

Have a jump-roping or pogo-stick-jumping contest. Can anyone get to seventy-seven?

Living It

Seventy-seven is a big number, isn't it? Jesus wasn't saying we should keep track of each time someone does something wrong to us; after all, every time we forgive, we try to forget. First Corinthians 13:5 says that love keeps no record of wrongs. Jesus was saying that we need to forgive again . . . and again . . . and again. He said to forgive repeatedly. The disciples asked for more faith to be able to do that. They realized they couldn't do it without God's help.

Discussion Question

◉ How can we forgive someone repeatedly?

Prayer Prompter

Please help us to forgive again and again and again.

Forgive and Forgive

Your Fellow Servant
Matthew 18:23-35

Memory Verse

"I canceled all that debt of yours because you begged me to. Shouldn't you have had mercy on your fellow servant just as I had on you?" (Matthew 18:32, 33).

Attention Grabber

Act out the following story from Matthew 18 with play money, or even real money: The king lends a lot of money to Servant 1. Servant 1 lends a little to Servant 2. Servant 1 begs the king to be patient till he can repay; the king feels sorry for him and forgives his debt. Servant 2 begs Servant 1 to be patient till he can repay, but Servant 1 will not. Servant 1 has Servant 2 punished severely. The king finds out and punishes Servant 1 severely, too.

Living It

God expects us to offer the same forgiveness and mercy to others that he has given us. When we're tempted to protest that the person who wronged us doesn't deserve our forgiveness, we need to remember that we don't deserve God's forgiveness either!

Discussion Questions

◎ Can you remember a time when God forgave you for something that you had felt very guilty about?
◎ Can your thankfulness for that help you to forgive someone who has done something wrong to you?

Prayer Prompter

Please help us to forgive as you have forgiven us.

What God Has Joined ...

Matthew 19:3-6

Memory Verse

"So they are no longer two, but one. Therefore what God has joined together, let man not separate" (Matthew 19:6).

Attention Grabber

Use food coloring in water, watercolor paints, or crayons to demonstrate what happens when colors are mixed. Ask the kids, "What happens when you combine yellow and blue? Yellow and red? Blue and red?" Explain that when two people marry, two become one.

Living It

Today's verse is part of some marriage ceremonies. When God joins two people in marriage, he doesn't want anything to break them apart. They are related to each other just as much as their children will be related to them. God wants married couples to stay in love with each other, treat one another with respect, forgive one another, and remain married. Jesus said divorce is only for some very extreme situations.

Discussion Question

◎ How can you keep your marriage strong someday?

Prayer Prompter

Please bless the children who are growing up right now that will marry the children in our family someday. Help them learn the value of a strong marriage, too. Bless us with good marriages and help us to keep them strong.

Let the Children Come

Matthew 19:14

Memory Verse
Jesus said, "Let the little children come to me, and do not hinder them, for the kingdom of heaven belongs to such as these" (Matthew 19:14).

Attention Grabber
Have the kids look in mirrors and draw portraits of themselves with Jesus. If desired, they can cut a frame from poster board and decorate it with paint pens, sequins, stickers, bright tissue paper scraps, old keys, ribbons tied into bows, or other items.

Living It
Even though Jesus was very busy sharing the gospel and helping people while he was on the earth, he was never too busy for children. He is still not too busy for you. Any time you come to him in prayer, he will listen to you.

Discussion Questions
◉ What are some things Jesus would like to hear about in your prayers?
◉ How can you remember to pray in the morning and in the evening?

Prayer Prompter
Thank you for loving us and wanting us to come to you. Please remind us to come to you when we're happy and when we're sad.

The Eye of the Needle
Matthew 19:24-26

Memory Verse
"Again I tell you, it is easier for a camel to go through the eye of a needle than for a rich man to enter the kingdom of God." When the disciples heard this, they were greatly astonished and asked, "Who then can be saved?" Jesus looked at them and said, "With man this is impossible, but with God all things are possible" (Matthew 19:24-26).

Attention Grabber
Let each family member try to thread a needle with embroidery floss (help them if necessary). Then let the kids sew their first and last initials on their washcloths. You can let younger children sew by threading yarn with masking tape around its tip through holes you have punched in a paper plate to form their initials.

Living It
Getting a thread through a needle isn't even easy, is it? Getting a camel through one would be impossible. But with God anything is possible. Jesus was saying that it's harder for wealthy people to humble themselves enough to follow Jesus as king. We need to make sure that no matter how much or how little we have, God is our first priority.

Discussion Question
◉ Why is it harder for rich people to follow Jesus? (They may think they don't need him, they may be proud and don't want to humble themselves, they don't want to share their wealth as Jesus commands, or they may want status and be embarrassed about being a Christian.)

Prayer Prompter
Please help us not to let money or anything else get in the way of us following Jesus as king.

God Rewards Sacrifices

Matthew 19:29

Memory Verse
"And everyone who has left houses or brothers or sisters or father or mother or children or fields for my sake will receive a hundred times as much and will inherit eternal life" (Matthew 19:29).

Attention Grabber
Show your kids how to gift wrap a box and lid (which you can use for an actual gift later). Tell them to imagine themselves putting everything they care about in that box as a gift to God. Encourage them to offer back to God everything he has given them.

Living It
Sometimes people have to make very difficult sacrifices to follow Jesus. Sometimes they may have to travel far from their homes and from people they love to preach the gospel. They might need to give up a career they like in order to serve Jesus all of the time. They might need to sell some of their possessions to give the money to help the needy or to build a church. Jesus says that no matter what you may sacrifice for him, you will receive back much more than he ever asks you to give.

Discussion Question
◎ Is there anything or anyone you cannot give to God? If so, why not?

Prayer Prompters
Please help us to trust you enough to offer to you everything you have given to us. Please use our lives and belongings however you want.

Take Your Pay and Go
Matthew 20:14, 15

Memory Verse

"Take your pay and go. I want to give the man who was hired last the same as I gave you. Don't I have the right to do what I want with my own money? Or are you envious because I am generous?" (Matthew 20:14, 15).

Attention Grabber

Sing a song that is in a round, such as "Row, Row, Row Your Boat." Emphasize that just as different people joined the song at different times, people join God's kingdom at different times.

Living It

The privilege of going to heaven is based on God's mercy and kindness, not how much work we have done. The robber who repented on the cross next to Jesus didn't have time to do anything good at all except to believe in Jesus, yet Jesus promised to meet him in paradise. We should be grateful for every minute that we have been in God's kingdom working for him, not jealous of those who will be with God even though they haven't been in his kingdom as long.

Discussion Questions

- How have you benefited from being in God's kingdom already?
- What work does God want you to be doing right now to help his kingdom?

Prayer Prompter

Please help us to rejoice every time anyone comes into your kingdom, knowing he or she will get to live with you someday just as we will.

His Life As a Ransom
Matthew 20:25-28; Mark 10:41-44

Memory Verse
"The Son of Man did not come to be served, but to serve, and to give his life as a ransom for many" (Matthew 20:28).

Attention Grabber
Explain that a ransom note is a note a kidnapper writes to demand payment, and a ransom is what someone pays to free a loved one. Give the kids an old magazine and let them cut out the letters of their names to paste on paper because Jesus has paid a ransom to free them.

Living It
Sin held us prisoner. We couldn't stop sinning and someone would have to pay for what we had done wrong. Jesus gave his life as a ransom to set us free from sin. He didn't come here to be treated like royalty; he came to help us. He wants us to help other people, too.

Discussion Question
- You don't have to answer aloud, but can you think of a sin that Jesus has helped you overcome?
- How can you use the talents God has given to you to serve others?

Prayer Prompter
Please help us to be sensitive to the needs of others. Help us do what we can to help.

Many Are Invited
Matthew 22:1-14

Memory Verse
"For many are invited, but few are chosen" (Matthew 22:14).

Attention Grabber
Beforehand, gather all of the family's robes or coats. As each family member enters the room, help him put on his robe. Tell your kids that Isaiah rejoiced because God clothed him with garments of salvation and dressed him in a robe of righteousness (Isaiah 61:10). When Joshua saw an angel, the angel had him take off his dirty clothes and put on clean ones as a symbol of having his sin taken away (Zechariah 3:3, 4).

Living It
Jesus told a parable about a king who invited many people to a wedding feast for his son, but only a few came. Of the ones who came, the only ones who could stay wore special wedding clothes the host gave them. God invites everyone into his kingdom, but the ones who can stay are those who let him clothe them in the garment of righteousness. Our righteousness (right standing with God) doesn't come through keeping the law; it comes through faith in Christ (Philippians 3:9). If it came through keeping God's laws, Christ would have died for nothing (Galatians 2:21). Romans 3:22 says, "This righteousness from God comes through faith in Jesus Christ to all who believe."

Discussion Questions
◉ Are you wearing the robe of righteousness?
◉ Do you feel clean through trusting Jesus to take away your sins?

Prayer Prompter
We need you so much, Lord. We can only be right with you through faith that Jesus' blood makes us clean. Help us to confess our sins to you rather than trying to ignore them or hide them. Help us trust you to take them away and give us a "robe of righteousness" because of Jesus' sacrifice for us.

Many Are Invited

Give God What Is God's
Matthew 22:19-21; Mark 12:15-17; Luke 20:25

Memory Verse
"Give to Caesar what is Caesar's, and to God what is God's"
(Matthew 22:21).

Attention Grabber
Read today's story aloud from Matthew 22:19-21. Make pennies shine like new by dropping them into a mixture of 4 tablespoons vinegar and 1 teaspoon salt. Then dry them and pitch pennies to see who can get them closest to a line of tape on the floor without crossing it.

Living It
Whose images are on our country's coins? The coin in today's story was made in Caesar's image. People were made in whose image? God's! (Genesis 1:26). Jesus was saying that we should pay our leaders the taxes that they require, but that we should give ourselves to God.

Discussion Question
◉ How can you give yourself to God?

Prayer Prompter
Please help us to give ourselves to you.

Know the Scriptures
Matthew 22:29; Mark 12:24

Memory Verse
Jesus replied, "You are in error because you do not know the Scriptures or the power of God" (Matthew 22:29).

Attention Grabber
Read a story directly from the Bible and have the kids read along in their Bibles (not storybooks). Misread some of the facts and pause to let the children correct you.

Living It
Although it is helpful to read Bible stories and listen to teachers who make the Bible easier to understand, it is very important to read from the Bible ourselves, too. We could believe things that aren't true if we don't know what the Bible really says and if we don't know God well enough to see his power in our daily lives.

Discussion Questions
◉ When is a good time of day for your personal Bible reading time?
◉ What could help our family members stay motivated to study?

Prayer Prompter
Please help us to know the truth by reading your Word and knowing you well enough to see your power in our daily lives.

Greatest Commandment
Matthew 22:36-38; Mark 12:29, 30

Memory Verse
Jesus replied: "'Love the Lord your God with all your heart and with all your soul and with all your mind.' This is the first and greatest commandment" (Matthew 22:37, 38).

Attention Grabber
Beforehand, spray paint old jigsaw puzzle pieces red and let them dry. Have your family cut large hearts out of poster board, write the verse on them, and glue puzzle pieces around the edges. Then use duct tape to attach a paper clip to the back for hanging. If you don't have puzzle pieces to decorate the hearts, just cut the hearts into jigsaw puzzles instead of using them as wall hangings.

Living It
What God wants from you more than anything else is your love. He doesn't want just a little of your love; he wants you to love him with your whole heart, soul, and mind. We need to get rid of whatever thoughts and feelings get in the way of loving God completely. As you come near to him, he'll come near to you (James 4:8).

Discussion Questions
- If we are angry at God, what should we do?
- How can we avoid being distracted from God by worries?
- If "to know him is to love him," how can we know God better?

Prayer Prompter
We love you. Please help us to rid our hearts, souls, and minds of anything that prevents us from loving you fully.

Love Your Neighbor

Matthew 22:39; Mark 12:31

Memory Verse

"And the second is like it: 'Love your neighbor as yourself'"
(Matthew 22:39).

Attention Grabber

Encourage your family to take this challenge: For a full day, every time you do something for yourself, offer to do it for someone else. For example, when you put toothpaste on your toothbrush, ask if anyone else would like some. When you pour your cereal, ask if anyone else would like a bowl, too. When sharpening a pencil for your homework, sharpen an extra and give it to someone else in the family.

Living It

After loving God, the most important commandment is to love the people around you as you love yourself. You love yourself enough to make sure you have what you need. God wants you to care about others that same way.

Discussion Questions

◉ Can you think of any of your behaviors that are selfish?
◉ How can you change them to selfless behaviors instead?

Prayer Prompter

Please help us to feel and show love to everyone around us.

It's All Right Here
Matthew 22:37-40

Memory Verse
"All the Law and the Prophets hang on these two commandments"
(Matthew 22:40).

Attention Grabber
Discuss how various commands show love for either God, people, or both. If you have time, create two simple windsocks made out of plastic report covers. Staple each cover to itself so that it forms a tube. Punch three holes in one end of each tube and tie twine through the holes. Gather the three pieces of twine together, and attach a fourth, longer piece which you will tie to a tree. Write "Love God" on one windsock and "Love Other People" on the other. Write different commandments on ribbons and discuss how keeping them shows love for God or others, and then staple them to the appropriate windsock. Hang the windsocks outside.

Living It
God has given you an easy way to remember his commandments. If you love God and people, you will be keeping all of the others because the others are all based on those two. Try to show love for God and people with every word and action, and you will be living the way God wants.

Discussion Question
◉ Which of your actions don't show love to God or other people?

Prayer Prompter
Please help us to decide what to do and say by whether the action and words show love for you and others.

Practice What You Preach
Matthew 23:3

Memory Verse
"So you must obey them and do everything they tell you. But do not do what they do, for they do not practice what they preach" (Matthew 23:3).

Attention Grabber
Play a variation of "Wheel of Fortune." On a piece of paper or a chalkboard, draw a blank for each letter of "Practice what you preach." If a person guesses a letter that is in the phrase, have him write the letter in the blank(s) and give him another turn. If he guesses incorrectly, it becomes the next player's turn. The first person to guess the phrase while it is his turn is the winner.

Living It
You've probably heard someone say, "Actions speak louder than words." When we try to tell people about Jesus, they will look at what we do more than what we say. If we say, "You can trust Jesus to take away your cares," they will look to see if we are worried. If we say, "When you ask Jesus to be your Lord, you need to let him change your life," they will look to see if our life is different from non-believers' lives. Others will believe us if we practice what we preach.

Discussion Questions
◎ What are some truths you would like to tell your friends about Jesus?
◎ Can they see those truths in your life?

Prayer Prompter
Please help us to practice what we preach.

Don't Swallow a Camel
Matthew 23:24

Memory Verse
"You blind guides! You strain out a gnat but swallow a camel"
(Matthew 23:24).

Attention Grabber
Beforehand, hide small candies in a bowl of sugar. Have one of the kids pour the sugar through a strainer into another bowl.

Living It
In Bible times, some of the people strained their water to prevent swallowing insects that were unclean. Jesus compared these people to people who lead others when they can't see what is important themselves. They care about nitpicky rules while overlooking giant sins in their lives.

Discussion Question
◉ While keeping nitpicky rules, do you overlook the most important commands to love God and people?

Prayer Prompter
Please help us to remember and obey the most important commands.

First Clean the Inside
Matthew 23:25, 26

Memory Verse
"Woe to you, teachers of the law and Pharisees, you hypocrites! You clean the outside of the cup and dish, but inside they are full of greed and self-indulgence. Blind Pharisee! First clean the inside of the cup and dish, and then the outside also will be clean" (Matthew 23:25, 26).

Attention Grabber
Beforehand, rub chocolate syrup inside tea cups and arrange the cups on a tray. Hold the tray up high so no one can see inside the cups. Announce that for a special treat, today you will drink out of your most beautiful cups. Lower the tray and when everyone expresses disgust about the dirty cups, explain that it is actually only chocolate. Stir milk into the cups and serve.

Living It
We all spend a lot of time trying to make ourselves look good on the outside. We wash our hair, blow-dry it, style it, and spray it. We brush our teeth. Some of us wear makeup and jewelry. We buy nice clothes, wash them, and iron them. We're careful about how our characters appear to others, too, trying to keep a good reputation. Jesus says it's much more important for us to take care of how we are on the inside. If we're genuinely beautiful on the inside, that will show through on the outside.

Discussion Question
◉ What kind of things make a person dirty on the inside like an unwashed cup?

Prayer Prompter
Please cleanse us from sin, Lord. Help us to remember that you are more concerned about our insides than our outsides.

First Clean the Inside

Whitewashed Tombs
Matthew 23:27, 28

Memory Verse
"In the same way, on the outside you appear to people as righteous but on the inside you are full of hypocrisy and wickedness" (Matthew 23:28).

Attention Grabber
Cut a mask out of a paper plate for each family member to decorate. Tape a pencil or stick to each mask. If you have time this week, drive through a cemetery with the kids and point out a pretty mausoleum.

Living It
Sometimes we act differently on the outside than we really are on the inside. It's as if we are wearing a mask. What is it called when we pretend to be following God on the outside but we really aren't? (hypocrisy). Jesus compared hypocrisy to a freshly-painted tomb full of rotting bones. First John 1:6 says, "If we claim to have fellowship with him yet walk in the darkness, we lie and do not live by the truth." First Chronicles 28:9 says that "the Lord searches every heart and understands every motive behind the thoughts."

Discussion Question
◉ Can you think of a way your inside self needs to match your outside self better?

Prayer Prompter
Please help us to be sincerely devoted to you.

Under a Hen's Wings
Matthew 23:37; Luke 13:34

Memory Verse

"O Jerusalem, Jerusalem, you who kill the prophets and stone those sent to you, how often I have longed to gather your children together, as a hen gathers her chicks under her wings, but you were not willing" (Matthew 23:37).

Attention Grabber

Set up an umbrella (a beach umbrella, a patio umbrella, or a personal rain umbrella) and have your devotion underneath it. If you have tiny paper umbrellas, serve glasses of fruit juice decorated with them.

Living It

What does an umbrella do for us? It protects us. Hens use their wings a little like umbrellas. They gather their chicks under their wings to protect them from a storm. Jesus told the people of Jerusalem that he had wanted to do that for them, too, but they weren't willing. Jesus wants to protect us and help us through the storms of life. When we run to him, we can count on him always to be there to help us and protect us.

Discussion Question

◉ How has Jesus helped you through rough times in the past?

Prayer Prompter

Thank you for wanting to help us and protect us. Help us to turn to you first when we face storms in our lives.

The World Will Hear
Matthew 24:14; Mark 13:10; Luke 24:47

Memory Verse

"And this gospel of the kingdom will be preached in the whole world as a testimony to all nations, and then the end will come" *(Matthew 24:14).*

Attention Grabber

Sing "Jesus Loves the Little Children" together. If you know a foreign language, sing the song in that language, too. If you have a globe or world atlas, cover the names of some of the countries with self-stick notes and have the kids guess them. (Give hints, such as talking with the accent of that country's people or mentioning a food that originated there.)

Living It

Jesus loves the little children, all the little children of the world. In fact, he is waiting to return until people in every country have had a chance to hear about him. He is patient because he wants everyone to have a chance to repent so they can live with him in heaven (2 Peter 3:9).

Discussion Questions

- How can we spread the gospel where we live?
- How can we help it spread to other countries?

Prayer Prompter

Please show us how you want us to spread the good news everywhere, and help us to be faithful to do what you ask.

As Lightning
Matthew 24:26, 27; Luke 17:24

Memory Verse
"For as lightning that comes from the east is visible even in the west, so will be the coming of the Son of Man" (Matthew 24:27).

Attention Grabber
If you have a sounds of nature recording of a thunderstorm, play it during today's devotion. Gather in a dark room and make Lifesaver Lightning by biting wintergreen Lifesavers hard candies. Go outside and teach the kids the four compass directions.

Living It
As we get closer to when Jesus will return, people will claim that he has already arrived. Some will even pretend to be Jesus by performing signs and miracles to try to trick people (Matthew 24:24). Jesus said not to believe them. The same way that we can see lightning all the way across the sky, we will be able to see Jesus in the sky when he returns.

Discussion Questions
◉ How would you feel if you looked up and saw Jesus coming in the sky this afternoon?
◉ Why would you feel that way?

Prayer Prompter
Please help us not to be fooled by people who say Jesus has already come.

Coming on the Clouds
Matthew 24:30, 31; Mark 13:26-37

Memory Verse

"They will see the Son of Man coming on the clouds of the sky, with power and great glory. And he will send his angels with a loud trumpet call, and they will gather his elect from the four winds, from one end of the heavens to the other" (Matthew 24:30, 31).

Attention Grabber

Lie down on a blanket outside and find shapes in the clouds together. (If it's not a sunny, partly cloudy day, remind the kids of times they have done that in the past.) Explain that Jesus will come in the clouds when he returns. If you have cotton balls, let the kids glue them near the bottom of a piece of blue construction paper. Give the kids colored chalk or crayons and have them draw Jesus coming on the clouds.

Living It

When Jesus comes on the clouds, he will send his angels to gather those who have trusted him as their Savior. Won't it be great to see Jesus face to face? (If any of your children have not accepted Jesus as Savior and Lord, this might be a good time to discuss it with them. You can turn to page 268 for help.)

Discussion Question

◎ When have you been excited to see someone return after a long trip? How do you think you'll feel when Jesus returns?

Prayer Prompter

Thank you for loving us enough to send your Son to take the punishment for our sins. We are sorry for the wrong things we have done. Please forgive us because of Jesus' sacrifice. We love you and want to be with you forever in heaven.

No One But the Father

Matthew 24:36; Mark 13:32

Memory Verse

"No one knows about that day or hour, not even the angels in heaven, nor the Son, but only the Father" (Matthew 24:36).

Attention Grabber

Set a kitchen timer and hide it. Say, "No one knows exactly when the timer will ring. Let's see who can find it before it does."

Living It

Some people have said they knew when Jesus was returning, and all of them were wrong. The Bible says that only God the Father knows the hour and the day when Jesus will return. Since we don't know exactly when it will be, we need to be prepared all of the time by keeping our relationship with God strong and doing the work he wants us to do.

Discussion Questions

◎ Do you feel ready to see Jesus?
◎ Why or why not?

Prayer Prompter

Please help us to be ready for Jesus' return.

Keep Watch!
Matthew 25:13; Mark 13:1-33

Memory Verse
"Therefore keep watch, because you do not know the day or the hour" (Matthew 25:13).

Attention Grabber
Sing "Give Me Oil in My Lamp" or "This Little Light of Mine." Tape together strips of paper to make a strip long enough to fit around the lampshade in each child's room. Have the kids write the verse on the strip, decorate it, and tape it around their lampshades.

Living It
Jesus said many times that he wants us to watch over our duties and be ready for his return. In the parable of the ten bridesmaids with lamps, he shows that we need to be ready for his return like the bridesmaids needed to have oil in their lamps. We can find guidance about how to prepare in 2 Peter 3. It says to live holy and godly lives (verse 11), "make every effort to be found spotless, blameless and at peace with him" (verse 14), "be on your guard so that you may not be carried away by the error of lawless men and fall from your secure position" (verse 17), and "grow in the grace and knowledge of our Lord and Savior Jesus Christ" (verse 18).

Discussion Question
◉ What would you do differently if you knew Jesus were coming one week from today?

Prayer Prompter
Please help us to be watchful and prepared for the return of our Savior.

Well Done!
Matthew 25:14-30; Luke 19:11-27

Memory Verse
"His master replied, 'Well done, good and faithful servant! You have been faithful with a few things; I will put you in charge of many things. Come and share your master's happiness!'" (Matthew 25:21).

Attention Grabber
Praise each family member for a special ability God has given that person. Ask how each can use that blessing for God.

Living It
God has given each of us many things—talents, gifts, knowledge, and more. He doesn't want us to just hold onto the things he entrusts to us until he returns. He wants us to increase them. If you see what God has entrusted to you, it gives you clues about how he wants you to serve him.

Discussion Questions
◉ What has God entrusted to you?
◉ How can you use those talents, gifts, and blessings to serve God?

Prayer Prompter
Please help us to faithfully serve you so that someday we will hear you say to us, "Well done!"

One of the Least
Matthew 25:31-46

Memory Verse

"The King will reply, 'I tell you the truth, whatever you did for one of the least of these brothers of mine, you did for me'" (Matthew 25:40).

Attention Grabber

Give your family choices of ways to serve Jesus by serving like the sheep in his story. Plan to do one of the following together within a week: Help the hungry and thirsty by working at or donating to the local food bank. Help strangers by taking a meal, phone number list, and homemade map to welcome new neighbors. Help those who need clothes by packing up your family's outgrown outfits for a less fortunate family or charity. Help the sick by running errands for a cancer patient or delivering coloring books to a children's hospital. Help prisoners by taking Bibles, Christian books, and magazines to a prison library.

Living It

Jesus loves everyone so much that whenever we do something kind for anyone, it's as if we did it for him. We don't need to limit our service to the kinds of things the sheep in his story did, but those are a good starting place. Sometimes it's easy to get caught up in our own lives; we need to reach beyond ourselves and help people in need around us.

Discussion Question

◎ How do you feel when you are helping others?

Prayer Prompter

Please help us to love people as much as you do. Help us to see the needs around us and fill them.

My Body and Blood

Matthew 26:26-29; Mark 14:22-25; Luke 22:19, 20

Memory Verse

While they were eating, Jesus took bread, gave thanks and broke it, and gave it to his disciples, saying, "Take and eat; this is my body." Then he took the cup, gave thanks and offered it to them, saying, "Drink from it, all of you. This is my blood of the covenant, which is poured out for many for the forgiveness of sins" (Matthew 26:26-28).

Attention Grabber

If your family would feel comfortable doing so, serve Communion in your home. You could read Matthew 26:26-28, pray, and then eat bread and drink grape juice. You could discuss how Communion is served at your church. Or discuss memorials and other ways we remember important events from our past.

Living It

When we look at bread and wine (or grape juice), they help us remember that Jesus sacrificed his body and blood for us. Because bread and wine were a part of daily life in Bible times, people would remember Jesus every day when they had their meals. First Corinthians 11:28, 29 says each of us should examine himself before he eats of the bread and drinks of the cup. Before we take Communion, we need to ask God's forgiveness for any sins for which we haven't already repented, and we need to be grateful for Jesus' sacrifice for us. (If your children have not yet become Christians and begun taking Communion, relate your own experiences. They will enjoy knowing what to expect.)

Discussion Question

◉ What do we remember about Jesus when we take Communion?

Prayer Prompter

Thank you for the sacrifice of your Son. Please help us to take Communion with a pure and grateful heart.

My Body and Blood

Matthew 26:36-46; Mark 14:38; Luke 22:45

Memory Verse

"Watch and pray so that you will not fall into temptation. The spirit is willing, but the body is weak" (Matthew 26:41).

Attention Grabber

Pretend to fall asleep in front of the kids. After they wake you, have them take turns seeing how well they can convince the others they're asleep. Ask if they have ever pretended to be asleep in the car to get carried into the house. Have they fallen asleep on their knees while praying?

Living It

Jesus' disciples had a real problem with sleepiness. They couldn't force themselves to stay awake during a very important time— while Jesus was praying to prepare for the cross. Jesus had wanted them to watch and pray so they could resist temptation, but they didn't because they were "exhausted from sorrow" (Luke 22:45). What temptation did they fall into? All the disciples deserted Jesus and ran away (Matthew 26:56).

Discussion Question

◉ What temptations are you facing right now that you need to watch and pray to be able to resist?

Prayer Prompter

Please help us to take control of our bodies, making our flesh obey what our spirits want to do. Help us to watch for the temptations that we will face and give us the strength to resist them. Help us to stay alert for whatever you want us to do.

It Must Happen This Way
Matthew 26:47-56

Memory Verse

"Do you think I cannot call on my Father, and he will at once put at my disposal more than twelve legions of angels? But how then would the Scriptures be fulfilled that say it must happen in this way?" (Matthew 26:53, 54).

Attention Grabber

Draw a face on an unpeeled potato. Cut two ears out of paper (or use two apricots) and attach them to the potato with toothpicks. Introduce this potato man as the high priest's servant, Malchus, who came with the soldiers to arrest Jesus and take him away. Ask the kids to show what Peter did to Malchus. (They should pretend to cut off an ear and pull it off of the potato.) Ask them to show what Jesus did. (They should reattach the ear.)

Living It

Jesus didn't need his disciples to protect him from the soldiers. He could have called an army of angels to help him. He had a choice about whether to die or not. No one took his life from him; he had the power to lay it down and take it up again (John 10:17, 18).

Discussion Question

◉ What would you have done if you were one of Jesus' disciples?

Prayer Prompter

We praise Jesus for being willing to lay down his life for us.

Make Disciples

Memory Verse

"Therefore go and make disciples of all nations, baptizing them in the name of the Father and of the Son and of the Holy Spirit, and teaching them to obey everything I have commanded you" (Matthew 28:19, 20).

Attention Grabber

Have the kids say hello in as many different languages as they can. Teach them a few more words that you know. If desired, make snacks from other countries, such as nachos from Mexico and Swiss cocoa from Switzerland. (For Quick Nachos, see recipe on page 267.)

Living It

Someday God may call us to go teach his gospel in another country, or he may have us teach it in our own country. He wants us to make disciples, or learners. He wants us to get people started learning from Jesus—reading the Bible and praying. He wants us to baptize them and teach them to obey him.

Discussion Question

◉ If God sent you to a foreign country to share his gospel, which country would you prefer and why?

Prayer Prompter

Help us to unselfishly share your gospel and inspire others to learn from you.

I Am Always With You
Matthew 28:20

Memory Verse
"And surely I am with you always, to the very end of the age"
(Matthew 28:20).

Attention Grabber
Make paper airplanes. Ask, "If you got on an airplane and flew far away, would Jesus be with you? If you got in a submarine and went to the bottom of the sea, would he be with you? What about if you flew in a rocket to the moon or a faraway planet?"

Living It
Psalm 139:7-10 says, "Where can I go from your Spirit? Where can I flee from your presence? If I go up to the heavens, you are there; if I make my bed in the depths, you are there. If I rise on the wings of the dawn, if I settle on the far side of the sea, even there your hand will guide me, your right hand will hold me fast." No matter where you go, Jesus is with you every minute of the day. You never have a reason to feel lonely!

Discussion Question
◎ In what situations does it strengthen you to know Jesus is with you?

Prayer Prompter
Help us always to be aware that Jesus is with us. Let that encourage us, comfort us, and help us to do your will.

Jesus Reached Out

Memory Verse

Filled with compassion, Jesus reached out his hand and touched the man. "I am willing," he said. "Be clean!" (Mark 1:41).

Attention Grabber

Dress as much like a movie star as you can (don't forget the sunglasses!). Ask the kids what Hollywood says people should look like. Emphasize that appearance is very important to many people, but not to God. God loves us all, no matter what we look like.

Living It

In Bible times, leprosy was a serious skin disease. Lepers had to live separate from people who did not have the disease. No one would touch them, except Jesus. First Samuel 16:7 says, "Man looks at the outward appearance, but the Lord looks at the heart." The leper said to Jesus, "If you are willing, you can make me clean." He had faith in Jesus' power to heal, and Jesus made his leprosy disappear immediately.

Discussion Questions

◉ Do you choose who to help based on what people look like?
◉ Do you believe Jesus has the power to heal?

Prayer Prompter

Thank you for reaching out to us, no matter what we look like. Please increase our faith in your power to heal.

Follow Me
Mark 2:13-17; Matthew 9:9; Luke 5:27, 28

Memory Verse

As he walked along, he saw Levi son of Alphaeus sitting at the tax collector's booth. "Follow me," Jesus told him, and Levi got up and followed him (Mark 2:14).

Attention Grabber

Say, "Follow me," and lead the kids in a quick game of "Follow-the-Leader." Comment on whether everyone responded quickly or hesitated.

Living It

Jesus said just two words to Levi (who is also called Matthew) and the man stood up and left his job. All Jesus said was "Follow me." Levi didn't hesitate or ask a lot of questions. Jesus didn't have to force him or persuade him. He wants us to respond that way, too. The tax collectors were some of the most hated people in Bible times, but Jesus asked one of them to be one of his disciples. You don't have to be popular for Jesus to want you in his kingdom.

Discussion Question

◎ What would you do if Jesus walked up to you while you were with your friends and said, "Follow me?" In a way, that's what the Holy Spirit says when we're doing something we shouldn't. Would you respond as Levi did?

Prayer Prompter

Please help us to follow you as Levi did.

Tell Your Family

Mark 5:1-20

Memory Verse

Jesus did not let him, but said, "Go home to your family and tell them how much the Lord has done for you, and how he has had mercy on you" (Mark 5:19).

Attention Grabber

Have the family make a gratitude chain of paper clips. Then have them take turns telling something God has done for them and adding a paper clip to the chain. Can they make one long enough to cross the room? Long enough to cross the house? If they enjoy the activity, add to the chain at dinner every night for a week.

Living It

Jesus made a drastic difference in the life of the man in today's story. When we get to know Jesus, he makes big improvements in us and our lives, too. He wants us to be open with our families about these things. Sometimes it is hard to share what he is doing in our lives, but it can be a real help and encouragement to the rest of the family.

Discussion Questions

◉ How does it help you to hear what Jesus is doing in your family's life?

◉ In what ways is your relationship with Jesus growing?

Prayer Prompter

Please help us to be open with each other about our relationship with you.

Just Believe
Mark 5:35-43

Memory Verse
Ignoring what they said, Jesus told the synagogue ruler, "Don't be afraid; just believe" (Mark 5:36).

Attention Grabber
Ask the kids what they would like to be when they grow up. Mention that in Bible times, some people worked as professional mourners who were paid to cry loudly when someone died. Have them pretend they are being interviewed for a job as a mourner. Tell them that in today's story mourners were at Jairus's house because his daughter had died.

Living It
Even though Jesus was in the midst of a big crowd, he took time to help Jairus. Even when our situations seem hopeless and it seems as though we've waited too long to ask the Lord for help, we need to follow his counsel: "Don't be afraid; just believe."

Discussion Question
◎ How does trusting Jesus help you not to be afraid?

Prayer Prompter
Please help us to bring all of our problems to you, no matter how hopeless they seem.

Keep Our Eyes on Jesus
Mark 6:45-52; Matthew 14:26, 27; John 6:15-21

Memory Verse
But when they saw him walking on the lake, they thought he was a ghost. They cried out, because they all saw him and were terrified. Immediately he spoke to them and said, "Take courage! It is I. Don't be afraid" (Mark 6:49, 50).

Attention Grabber
Let the kids toss grapes or popcorn into the air and try to catch them in their mouths. Emphasize that they had to keep their eyes on the popcorn to be able to do the trick. Remind them that in sports they have to keep their eyes on the ball. In life we have to keep our eyes on Jesus.

Living It
In the story, Peter took his eyes off of Jesus and he began to sink. When we get distracted from focusing on Jesus, we start to sink into our cares. Sometimes people call getting things done and taking care of things "staying on top of things" or "staying afloat." The only way we can really do that is to keep our eyes on Jesus—look to him as our example and our help.

Discussion Question
◎ What distracts you from keeping your eyes on Jesus?

Prayer Prompter
Please help us not to get distracted from trusting you and following you.

Worship in Truth

Mark 7:6, 7

Memory Verse

He replied, "Isaiah was right when he prophesied about you hypocrites; as it is written: 'These people honor me with their lips, but their hearts are far from me. They worship me in vain; their teachings are but rules taught by men'" (Mark 7:6, 7).

Attention Grabber

Play "Two Truths and a Lie." Choose someone and instruct that person to say two true statements and one false statement. Can other family members tell which of the three statements is the false one?

Living It

Hypocrisy is when we praise God with our mouths, but our hearts aren't close to him. He wants our hearts to be pure, so we aren't pretending to love him. This is the only way our worship will honor him. This verse also stresses that it's important to teach what God really says in the Bible rather than just what people have made up.

Discussion Question

◉ Do the feelings in your heart match what your lips are saying about God?

Prayer Prompter

Please make our hearts clean so they match what we say with our mouths.

Worship in Truth

Out of Our Hearts

Memory Verse
"For from within, out of men's hearts, come evil thoughts, sexual immorality, theft, murder, adultery, greed, malice, deceit, lewdness, envy, slander, arrogance and folly. All these evils come from inside and make a man 'unclean'" (Mark 7:21-23).

Attention Grabber
Use colored chalk to draw a heart on a sheet. Have everyone place three rolled pairs of socks in the heart on the sheet. Tell the kids that the socks represent the evil thoughts in our hearts (name them from the verse). Have them hold the edges of the sheet and try to make their own socks fly out of the heart and sheet without flipping out anyone else's. The first person whose socks are out of the heart is the winner.

Living It
We think of doing bad things before we actually do them. Jesus wants us to resist temptations (desires to do bad things) long before they turn into actions, instead of thinking about the bad things until we do them.

Discussion Question
◉ Do you see any of those temptations from the memory verse growing in your heart? (You don't have to answer aloud, but think carefully.)

Prayer Prompter
Please remove temptations that are growing in our hearts.

Betrayed, Crucified, Risen

Mark 9:30, 31

Memory Verse
"The Son of Man is going to be betrayed into the hands of men. They will kill him, and after three days he will rise" (Mark 9:31).

Attention Grabber
Beforehand, put any small object (such as a snack, pencil, or sticker) into a paper sack for each child. Staple the bag shut and draw a question mark on it. Ask the kids if they can guess what is inside the grab bags. Ask if God knows. Explain that God knows everything, including the future.

Living It
Jesus knew ahead of time what would happen to him, yet he bravely faced it. Surprisingly, his followers didn't remember that Jesus had warned them about these events until an angel reminded them after Jesus rose from the dead (Luke 24:6-8). If his followers had realized these events were part of God's plan, they might not have panicked when the events happened.

Discussion Questions
- Have you ever reread a Bible story and been surprised by something that you had forgotten?
- Are you trusting God to take care of you in the future?

Prayer Prompter
Help us to trust that you have a plan for us and that you will always take care of us. Help us to face trials courageously.

The Servant of All

Mark 9:35

Memory Verse

Sitting down, Jesus called the Twelve and said, "If anyone wants to be first, he must be the very last, and the servant of all" (Mark 9:35).

Attention Grabber

Beforehand, do something of service for each family member. Can the others guess what it was? Challenge everyone to serve each member of the family within 24 hours. If you have removable stickers or self-stick notes on hand, give the kids one for each member of the family so they can leave the stickers behind as a hint that service happened in that spot.

Living It

If you want to make a difference in the world, make it by improving the lives of others. The truly great people are the ones who spend their lives helping others. Aren't the kindest, most loving, and most Christ-like people you know people who show that they care about others by serving them? What kind of things do those people do?

Discussion Question

◉ How can you use the talents God has given you to serve others?

Prayer Prompter

Please help us to be sensitive to the needs of others and to do what we can to help.

Whatever You Ask
Mark 11:24

Memory Verse
"Therefore I tell you, whatever you ask for in prayer, believe that you have received it, and it will be yours" (Mark 11:24).

Attention Grabber
Let the kids make prayer notebooks. They can decorate spiral notebooks or fold over pieces of paper and staple them together along the fold to make a notebook. Let them decorate the covers.

Living It
When we pray, we need to ask God to make our desires match what he wants. If we are sure that what we ask for is God's will, we can be sure that he will give us what we ask. Keep a record of what you have prayed about and write down when the answers come. It will be encouraging to you as you see how faithful God is to hear and answer your prayers. James 4:2, 3 says, "You do not have, because you do not ask God. When you ask, you do not receive, because you ask with wrong motives, that you may spend what you get on your pleasures."

Discussion Question
◉ Can you think of a prayer request you had that God answered recently?

Prayer Prompter
Please help us to trust you to faithfully answer our prayers.

The Widow's Mite

Mark 12:43, 44; Luke 21:1-4

Memory Verse

Calling his disciples to him, Jesus said, "I tell you the truth, this poor widow put more into the treasury than all the others. They all gave out of their wealth; but she, out of her poverty, put in everything—all she had to live on" (Mark 12:43, 44).

Attention Grabber

Make a game of standing on a chair and trying to drop pennies into a cup, jar, or can. (Let younger children kneel on the chair.) If you have time, let each child decorate a cup, jar, or can as a bank to hold his or her offerings.

Living It

The widow we read about didn't give a lot of money, but it was all she had. Jesus loved her attitude and faith. Her offering meant more to God than the bigger offerings because she gave with trust that God would take care of her. God wants us to listen to our hearts about what to give, and to give because we want to, not because we are forced to. Second Corinthians 9:7 says, "Each man should give what he has decided in his heart to give, not reluctantly or under compulsion, for God loves a cheerful giver."

Discussion Question

◉ How do you feel when you give money back to God?

Prayer Prompter

Please help us to see that everything we have is really yours. Show us what you want us to give, and help us to give it gladly.

Not What I Will
Mark 14:36; Matthew 26:39-42; Luke 22:42

Memory Verse
"Abba, Father," he said, *"everything is possible for you. Take this cup from me. Yet not what I will, but what you will"* (Mark 14:36).

Attention Grabber
Have all your family members copy the verse onto a strip of paper and tape it around a cup that they can keep in their room for a few days to remind them of what Jesus did. Emphasize that the "cup" was the suffering Jesus would experience when he took on our sins and was separated from God while on the cross.

Living It
"What you will" is another way of saying "what you want." Jesus was saying that he cared more about God the Father's desires than his own. We need to know God's plan for us and be willing to do what God wants, even when it is difficult.

Discussion Question
◉ What has the Holy Spirit asked you to do that was difficult for you?

Prayer Prompter
Please help us to know your will and do it.

The Great Commission

Memory Verse

"Go into all the world and preach the good news to all creation. Whoever believes and is baptized will be saved, but whoever does not believe will be condemned" (Mark 16:15, 16).

Attention Grabber

If you have baptismal certificates and photographs, look at them with the kids. Consider letting everyone help to frame them. Talk about why you or members of your family were baptized.

Living It

Jesus wants us to tell all people the good news that he died for them so they could be forgiven of their sins and live forever with God. He will save all of us from punishment for our sins if we believe in him. Baptism is a way to show that we have trusted Jesus to wash away our sins. Acts 22:16 says, "And now what are you waiting for? Get up, be baptized and wash your sins away, calling on his name." Colossians 2:12, 13 says that we have "been buried with him in baptism and raised with him through your faith in the power of God, who raised him from the dead. When you were dead in your sins . . . God made you alive with Christ. He forgave us all our sins."

Discussion Questions

- Has everyone in our extended family believed and been baptized?
- What are ways we can share the good news with aunts, uncles, cousins, and other family members? (Tell them, write letters, draw pictures.)

Prayer Prompter

Please help everyone in our family to believe in Jesus and be baptized. Please help us to share your good news with them and others.

Signs of Believers
Mark 16:17

Memory Verse
"And these signs will accompany those who believe" (Mark 16:17).

Attention Grabber
Beforehand, cut a doorknob sign out of poster board for each family member using the pattern on page 264. Let the kids decorate the signs however they wish.

Living It
A sign lets people know something important. Miracles can be signs that let people know we're believers by showing God's power in our lives. Dramatic miracles probably won't happen in our lives every day, but if we have a relationship with God and we watch for what he is doing, we'll see him at work daily.

Discussion Question
- What are some of the things God has been doing in your life lately?

Prayer Prompter
Please help us to have faith for you to do the miracles we need.

Signs of Believers

Love Your Enemies
Luke 6:27, 28

Memory Verse
"But I tell you who hear me: Love your enemies, do good to those who hate you, bless those who curse you, pray for those who mistreat you" *(Luke 6:27, 28).*

Attention Grabber
Have the children help you change the endings of a couple fairy tales so that the characters reform the villain by being kind to him.

Living It
When people hate, abuse, or mistreat us, it would be easy to want to hate, abuse, or mistreat them in return. But that's not what God wants. God loves everyone, and he wants us to love everyone, too—even those who mistreat us. As we pray for them, he replaces our bad feelings with love.

Discussion Question
◉ Can you think of someone who mistreats you for whom you can pray?

Prayer Prompter
Please help the people who mistreat us to feel your love. Help us to love them, forgive them, and treat them well.

The Golden Rule
Luke 6:31

Memory Verse
"Do to others as you would have them do to you" (Luke 6:31).

Attention Grabber
Have the kids each do an impersonation of what they would teach a parrot to say to them if they had one. Point out that no one would teach the parrot to insult them. Emphasize that we know how we want our pets, family, and friends to treat us.

Living It
We know how we want others to treat us—with kindness and love. That's the way God wants us to treat others. It's easy for us to know the right way to behave toward others by simply thinking about how we would want them to treat us.

Discussion Question
◉ Why do you think today's verse is called the Golden Rule?

Prayer Prompter
Please help us to treat others with the kindness and love that we would want them to show us.

Do Not Judge
Luke 6:37

Memory Verse
"Do not judge, and you will not be judged. Do not condemn, and you will not be condemned. Forgive, and you will be forgiven" (Luke 6:37).

Attention Grabber
Play with a yo-yo together. Emphasize that what you send out comes back.

Living It
The way we treat others will come back to us. Doesn't it feel awful when others have judged you and labeled you something negative? You may feel discouraged if people won't give you a chance. God doesn't want us to make others feel that way. Instead of judging, we can pray for them, reveal our own weaknesses, and encourage them.

Discussion Questions
◉ Why does God want us to love other people?
◉ How can you keep from being judgmental and condemning?

Prayer Prompter
Help me to be loving and accepting of other people. Help me to give them the same grace you give to me.

The Measure You Use

Luke 6:38

Memory Verse
"Give, and it will be given to you. A good measure, pressed down, shaken together and running over, will be poured into your lap. For with the measure you use, it will be measured to you" (Luke 6:38).

Attention Grabber
Place a set of measuring cups and spoons on the table. Let each person choose which measuring cup to use to measure juice for another family member. Then tell the kids the glass they poured is actually for themselves.

Living It
God is anxious to bless you. He'll reward you abundantly for every kindness you show to others. Freely pour out your love, acceptance, forgiveness, and help.

Discussion Questions
- Did you hope one of the bigger cups was for you?
- Is there someone the Holy Spirit has wanted you to treat with more kindness?

Prayer Prompter
Thank you for wanting to bless us. Please help us to be generous in pouring out your love and mercy to others.

Love Much
Luke 7:47

Memory Verse
"Therefore, I tell you, her many sins have been forgiven—for she loved much. But he who has been forgiven little loves little" (Luke 7:47).

Attention Grabber
Draw a bull's-eye target on paper and tape it to a wall. Wad masking tape into balls with the sticky side out. Have everyone stand behind a line and try to throw the balls at the target.

Living It
The word "sin" comes from archery. Sin was a term used to describe what happened when an archer shot an arrow and the arrow fell short of the target. If we had a pile of all the sins we have committed, it would be very high. When we think about our many sins, we can appreciate how gracious God has been to forgive us and love us. We love him deeply in return.

Discussion Question
◉ Have you ever felt guilty and then had those emotions washed away when you prayed?

Prayer Prompter
We love you, Lord. Thank you for forgiving us and loving us.

No Place to Lay His Head
Luke 9:57, 58

Memory Verse
"Foxes have holes and birds of the air have nests, but the Son of Man has no place to lay his head" (Luke 9:58).

Attention Grabber
Fill a plastic berry basket with nest-building materials (dryer lint, string, or tiny fabric scraps) and place it in a tree where birds can help themselves to it. Or simply look for a bird's nest in your backyard together.

Living It
During the three years of his ministry, Jesus traveled too much to have a home of his own. In this verse, he was telling people who say they will follow him that it isn't easy. When we're serving Jesus, sometimes we might not have a comfortable bed with a soft pillow. We might not have as much money as we want. We might not live where we would have chosen. Jesus will ask us to make sacrifices, but they are well worth it. Nothing compares with the peace that we have when we know we are right where God wants us and we're doing exactly what he wants us to do.

Discussion Question
◉ Is there any comfort you wouldn't be willing to give up to serve God?

Prayer Prompter
Help us to follow you, no matter what sacrifices you ask of us.

Don't Look Back
Luke 9:62

Memory Verse

"No one who puts his hand to the plow and looks back is fit for service in the kingdom of God" (Luke 9:62).

Attention Grabber

Have a wheelbarrow race. Then ask the kids how they would feel if they were the wheelbarrow part and the person steering them was looking back over his or her shoulder. That could be disastrous, couldn't it?

Living It

When we commit to serve God, it's like putting our hand to a plow that digs in the soil to get it ready for seeds. Looking back at our old life and rethinking our decision to follow Jesus is like looking over our shoulder. Just as a farmer can't do a good job if he doesn't keep looking straight ahead of him, we can't do a good job for God if we keep thinking about returning to our sin and selfishness.

Discussion Questions

◉ How have you put your hand to the plow?
◉ Have you started serving God in some way, then looked back? What happened?

Prayer Prompter

Please help us to be fully committed to serving you. Help us resist temptations to go back to the way we were before we followed you.

Sitting at Jesus' Feet
Luke 10:38-42

Memory Verse
"Martha, Martha," the Lord answered, "you are worried and upset about many things, but only one thing is needed. Mary has chosen what is better, and it will not be taken away from her" (Luke 10:41, 42).

Attention Grabber
Let the kids spin around in circles. Then explain that sometimes our lives get too busy and we feel as if we're spinning around in circles. If we get too busy, sometimes we can forget what's most important. We might even think we're too busy to pray.

Living It
Martha got so busy serving that she forgot who she was serving: Jesus Christ! She was about to pick a fight with her sister rather than listen to the Son of God! She called him Lord, but then she told *him* what to do. Maybe Jesus said her name twice because that's what it took to get her attention! When we're trying to get a lot done, we need to be careful not to get too busy to spend time listening to Jesus. When we get worried and upset like Martha, it is good to remember that Jesus said only one thing is needed: to sit at his feet. It is easy to get caught up in all of the cares of our life, but what matters more than anything is that we take time to pray and listen to God.

Discussion Question
◎ How does praying help you?

Prayer Prompter
Help us to remember that sitting at your feet is what matters more than whatever worries us.

Sitting at Jesus' Feet

Your Eye Is the Lamp
Luke 11:34, 35

Memory Verse
"Your eye is the lamp of your body. When your eyes are good, your whole body also is full of light. But when they are bad, your body also is full of darkness. See to it, then, that the light within you is not darkness" (Luke 11:34, 35).

Attention Grabber
Beforehand, close the blinds or curtains and turn out the lights. Gather everyone for the devotion. When someone mentions that it's awfully dark, emphasize that we need light. Say, "Jesus is the light, and we need him, too." Then turn on a lamp or open the window coverings.

Living It
Jesus said, "I am the light of the world" (John 8:12). In heaven the sun and moon don't need to shine because "the glory of God gives it light, and the Lamb is its lamp" (Revelation 21:23). What are some reasons we need light? Do we need Jesus for those same reasons?

Discussion Questions
- Do you see God's light in your life? How does it brighten your day when you're aware of his presence?
- Are you relying on Jesus to save you?

Prayer Prompter
Help us to have your light in our lives every day.

A Tenth of Your Mint
Luke 11:42

Memory Verse

"Woe to you Pharisees, because you give God a tenth of your mint, rue and all other kinds of garden herbs, but you neglect justice and the love of God. You should have practiced the latter without leaving the former undone" (Luke 11:42).

Attention Grabber

If you have mint leaves and chocolate chips, microwave the chocolate and paint it on the leaves. Refrigerate them, and then peel off the mint. Eat the chocolate leaves or use them to decorate a dessert. If you don't have mint leaves, measure out ten equal portions of another spice in front of the kids and drop one portion into an envelope labeled "tithe". Ask the kids if they think the church would like to receive this.

Living It

In Bible times, sometimes Pharisees prided themselves on tithing so thoroughly that they even gave a tenth of their spices, yet they didn't care about the way they treated people or the relationship they had with God. God doesn't want us to focus more on keeping rules than we do on being fair with others and loving God. Jesus didn't say people could recognize his disciples by their many rules; he said people will know we follow him if we love one another (John 13:35).

Discussion Questions

◉ Do people know that you love God?
◉ How can they tell?

Prayer Prompter

Help us to treat people fairly and show our love for you.

A Tenth of Your Mint

Lift a Finger to Help
Luke 11:46

Memory Verse

Jesus replied, "And you experts in the law, woe to you, because you load people down with burdens they can hardly carry, and you your-selves will not lift one finger to help them" (Luke 11:46).

Attention Grabber

How many cans of soup in a plastic grocery bag can each family member lift with one finger? Will the kids be willing to lift a finger to help carry the groceries in when you go shopping?

Living It

God wants us to be considerate. It's important to think about what work and worries we cause others, and to try to help however we can.

Discussion Questions

- What burdens do you put on your family, friends, and teachers?
- How can you help?

Prayer Prompter

Please show us how to be more considerate and helpful.

Guard Against Hypocrisy

Luke 12:1

Memory Verse
"Be on your guard against the yeast of the Pharisees, which is hypocrisy" (Luke 12:1).

Attention Grabber
Beforehand, remove sticks of gum from their wrappers and put the wrappers back into the pack. Offer the kids a stick of gum and give them an empty wrapper. When they look disappointed, give them the actual gum and say, "Be what you seem."

Living It
Hypocrisy is pretending to be something good on the outside that you aren't on the inside. God wants us to be genuine with other people. He wants us to admit our faults and how much we need God's forgiveness. He doesn't want us to be fake and puffed up. He wants us to let him purify us on the inside, rather than just pretending to be pure on the outside.

Discussion Questions
- How would you feel around a hypocrite?
- Would anyone consider you a hypocrite? Why or why not?

Prayer Prompter
Help us to be genuine with other people. Help us to be honest about how much we need your forgiveness. Please purify us so that we will be as good on the inside as we have tried to appear on the outside.

No Secrets
Luke 12:2, 3

Memory Verse

"There is nothing concealed that will not be disclosed, or hidden that will not be made known. What you have said in the dark will be heard in the daylight, and what you have whispered in the ear in the inner rooms will be proclaimed from the roofs" (Luke 12:2, 3).

Attention Grabber

Have the kids write the first line of the verse with white crayon. Then make it appear by painting over the words with watercolors. Or have them write the first line of the verse with a toothpick dipped in lemon juice. Then make it appear by holding it near a light bulb. Emphasize that what is hidden now will be seen when Jesus returns.

Living It

If you have any secrets, make sure they're ones you wouldn't be ashamed for the whole world to know. Someday everything will be out in the open. What we do in private needs to be as wholesome as what we do in public. What we think needs to be as pure as what we say. Romans 2:16 says, "God will judge men's secrets through Jesus Christ." First Corinthians 4:5 says, "He will bring to light what is hidden in darkness and will expose the motives of men's hearts." God knows our good secrets and will reward them (Matthew 6:4).

Discussion Question

◉ Do you have hidden sins that you need for God to get rid of?

Prayer Prompter

We know that you see everything in our lives. Help us to live so that we won't be ashamed when everyone else sees and hears it all, too. Please take away all of our sins, including our hidden ones.

The Holy Spirit
Luke 12:11, 12; Mark 13:11; John 14:26

Memory Verse
"When you are brought before synagogues, rulers and authorities, do not worry about how you will defend yourselves or what you will say, for the Holy Spirit will teach you at that time what you should say" *(Luke 12:11, 12).*

Attention Grabber
Give the kids alphabet cereal or alphabet soup. Have them find the letters to spell HE PUTS THE WORDS IN YOUR MOUTH.

Living It
Second Timothy 4:2 says, "Preach the Word; be prepared in season and out of season." First Peter 3:15 says, "Always be prepared to give an answer to everyone who asks you to give the reason for the hope that you have." We need to be prepared to talk to others about Jesus and to defend our beliefs, but we don't have to worry because the Holy Spirit will help us. He'll give us the words to say right when we need them.

Discussion Question
◎ In what situation have you felt that the Holy Spirit was helping you know what to say?

Prayer Prompter
Please help us to trust your Holy Spirit to help us when we tell others about you.

Guard Against Greed
Luke 12:15

Memory Verse

Then he said to them, "Watch out! Be on your guard against all kinds of greed; a man's life does not consist in the abundance of his possessions" (Luke 12:15).

Attention Grabber

Write or type on the computer "My Life" in outline letters on a piece of paper for each family member. Have the kids draw pictures inside the letters of the things that matter most in their life. Emphasize that some people would draw all of their possessions; however, what is most important can't be bought with money.

Living It

There is a lot of pressure in our society to crave belongings. Commercials try to convince us we need this product or that one. Kids at school act as if you must have the newest fad in toys or clothes to be cool. Some people act as though a person's worth is determined by how much his belongings cost. God wants us to be careful not to be greedy, because our lives aren't made of how many things we own.

Discussion Questions

- Have you ever bought something that was almost worthless to you once you got it home?
- What matters more to you than belongings? Why?

Prayer Prompter

Help us to spend our time and money on more important things than possessions.

Be Rich Toward God
Luke 12:16-21

Memory Verse
"But God said to him, 'You fool! This very night your life will be demanded from you. Then who will get what you have prepared for yourself?' This is how it will be with anyone who stores up things for himself but is not rich toward God" (Luke 12:20, 21).

Attention Grabber
Flip TV channels to commercials and act silly and crazed, saying things like, "I want it!" and "Gotta have it!" Point out that the TV shows are paid for by companies that want to sell you their products. Emphasize that no matter how much people have, commercials try to convince viewers that they need more. If you have time, drive through a less affluent neighborhood than yours to show your children that everyone doesn't have as much as they do.

Living It
If we spend all of our lives trying to get rich and spend money only on ourselves, we will waste it. God doesn't want us to spend all of our thoughts, time, money, and energy buying bigger and better things for ourselves. He wants us to serve him with our thoughts, time, money, and energy instead. For every good thing we do, God stores up rewards for us in heaven; that is how we become rich toward God.

Discussion Question
◉ What have you spent money on lately that wasn't for yourself?

Prayer Prompter
Please help us to spend our thoughts, time, money, and energy serving you.

Give to the Poor

Memory Verse

"Do not be afraid, little flock, for your Father has been pleased to give you the kingdom. Sell your possessions and give to the poor. Provide purses for yourselves that will not wear out, a treasure in heaven that will not be exhausted, where no thief comes near and no moth destroys" (Luke 12:32-34).

Attention Grabber

Gather a few unwanted items that are lying around your home to show the kids that you have more than you need. See if the family would like to have a garage sale and give the money to the poor, or if they would like to donate the items directly. Ask them if there are other items that they think they would be willing to give to others who need them more.

Living It

If we keep treasures here, they get worn out, stolen, or damaged. If we have treasures in heaven, they wait for us. Jesus is telling us to live modestly and to use our extra money and belongings to help the poor. God will reward us for everything we give.

Discussion Question

◎ Why are treasures in heaven better than treasures on earth?

Prayer Prompter

Please help us not to treasure our belongings. Help us to be generous with what you have given to us.

Surprise!
Luke 12:40

Memory Verse

"You also must be ready, because the Son of Man will come at an hour when you do not expect him" (Luke 12:40).

Attention Grabber

Let the kids put pantyhose legs over their faces like thieves. Explain that Jesus "will come like a thief in the night" (1 Thessalonians 5:2) and ask what that means (when most people don't expect him). If desired, take their pictures with a camera or video camera.

Living It

God is the only one who knows the exact date of Jesus' return. He wants us to be ready all the time. To be prepared, we need to accept Jesus as Savior and Lord ourselves, have our hearts pure before God, stay in a close relationship with him, let him guide us, and tell people about Jesus so they can be prepared, too.

Discussion Questions

- ◎ If you knew someone would throw you a surprise party but you didn't know when and where, how would you prepare?
- ◎ How is your preparation different for the surprise when the Lord returns?

Prayer Prompter

Help us to be ready for Jesus' return.

Bad Things Happen

Memory Verse

"Or those eighteen who died when the tower in Siloam fell on them— do you think they were more guilty than all others living in Jerusalem? I tell you, no! But unless you repent, you too will all perish" (Luke 13:4, 5).

Attention Grabber

Make a tower of blocks, cards, coins, books, or anything else stackable. Keep stacking until it tumbles. Explain that the tower in Siloam also fell.

Living It

When bad things happen, don't assume that someone did something wrong and is being punished. Bad things happen for many reasons. Try to empathize and sympathize with people who go through trials. Colossians 3:12 says to "clothe yourselves with compassion" and Romans 12:15 says to "mourn with those who mourn." Instead of judging other people, we need to examine our own hearts. Someday everyone will die, but only those who have forgiveness through Jesus will live forever with God.

Discussion Question

- How would you feel if you were going through a hard time and someone said it was punishment for your sins?

Prayer Prompter

Help us not to make suffering people feel worse by saying that they deserved what happened. Help us to be loving and compassionate to people who are going through trials. Please forgive our sins.

The Place of Honor
Luke 14:7-11

Memory Verse

"When someone invites you to a wedding feast, do not take the place of honor, for a person more distinguished than you may have been invited" (Luke 14:8).

Attention Grabber

Fold index cards in half crosswise and let the kids decorate them as place cards. Talk about how sometimes a host or hostess has special places where the guests are supposed to sit.

Living It

If you went to a wedding or other event and picked the fanciest chair for yourself, you might be embarrassed to find out that it was for someone else. Jesus is saying that we shouldn't assume that we deserve honor or try to get honor for ourselves. He will give honor to those who humble themselves.

Discussion Questions

◎ What are some behaviors that indicate we're getting too proud?

◎ Has God ever given you honor when you weren't seeking it for yourself?

Prayer Prompter

Please keep us humble, Lord.

Those Who Can't Repay

Memory Verse

"But when you give a banquet, invite the poor, the crippled, the lame, the blind, and you will be blessed. Although they cannot repay you, you will be repaid at the resurrection of the righteous" (Luke 14:13, 14).

Attention Grabber

Plan a simple get-together (perhaps even just a video and popcorn). Have each of the kids be sure to include a guest who is less fortunate, handicapped, or who doesn't have many friends.

Living It

God loves everyone, even those who are sometimes rejected by other people. He will bless us if we reach out and make friends with people who aren't accepted by others and who are unable to repay us. Remember that being kind to other people isn't an honor for them; it's an honor for us. Don't look down on them; look up to them.

Discussion Questions

◉ Why is it wrong to leave out people who are poor or handicapped?

◉ How can you include people whom others leave out?

Prayer Prompter

Please help us to show your love to people who are sometimes rejected.

Count the Cost
Luke 14:25-35

Memory Verse

"Suppose one of you wants to build a tower. Will he not first sit down and estimate the cost to see if he has enough money to complete it?" (Luke 14:28).

Attention Grabber

Tell the kids they get to make towers with mini-marshmallows or gumdrops and toothpicks. Ask them to figure out how many they will need of each to make a three-story tower. Then give them the number they request.

Living It

Following Jesus isn't something someone should stop doing once started. Jesus wants people to carefully consider what they are getting themselves into before they become Christians. When someone commits to follow Jesus as Lord, she is promising to follow him for the rest of her life and to give him whatever he asks. It is well worth it!

Discussion Questions

◉ What does it cost to follow Jesus?
◉ How is it worth the sacrifice?

Prayer Prompter

Please help us to keep serving you without stopping. Help us to be honest with others about the kind of commitment you want.

A Lost Silver Coin

Memory Verse

"Or suppose a woman has ten silver coins and loses one. Does she not light a lamp, sweep the house and search carefully until she finds it?" (Luke 15:8).

Attention Grabber

Hide nickels or quarters and let the children find them. For fun, you can let them look for coins that were minted the year they were born and let them do foil rubbings by placing foil over the coins and rubbing with their finger until the image appears.

Living It

In the story, the woman's coins were silver, which is very valuable. We're all very valuable to God. If one of us is lost in sin, God doesn't just say, "Oh well, I still have plenty of others." He won't give up on us. He wants us back with him again.

Discussion Question

◉ Do you feel as though you are valuable to God? Why or why not?

Prayer Prompter

Thank you for loving us and believing that we are of value. Help us not to get lost in sin.

Welcome Home!

Luke 15:11-32

Memory Verse

"So he got up and went to his father. But while he was still a long way off, his father saw him and was filled with compassion for him; he ran to his son, threw his arms around him and kissed him" (Luke 15:20).

Attention Grabber

Act out the story of the Lost Son from Luke 15:11-32. If you have time, have the kids make rings like the father gave his son. They can twist chenille stems into rings. Tape candy to the rings for "gems."

Living It

Today's story may be the best one ever told. Many people run from God rather than to him because they don't know that he is like the father in this story. God loves each of us deeply. When we sin, he doesn't want us to stay away; he wants us to repent and run into his arms. No matter what you do, God will always love you.

Discussion Question

◉ Picture God with his arms open to you. How does that picture make you feel?

Prayer Prompter

Thank you for loving us and wanting to be our Father. Help us not to avoid you when we have done wrong things.

Trustworthy With Riches

Luke 16:10, 11

Memory Verse

"Whoever can be trusted with very little can also be trusted with much, and whoever is dishonest with very little will also be dishonest with much. So if you have not been trustworthy in handling worldly wealth, who will trust you with true riches?" (Luke 16:10, 11).

Attention Grabber

Make a job chart together that lists amounts of money the kids can earn for various chores. Discuss ways to earn, tithe, save, and spend wisely.

Living It

God gives us all of the money that we have. What we do with his resources shows a lot about us. Do we work for it honestly? Do we save and spend it wisely? Are we generous in giving to the church and people in need? Learning to take good care of what God trusts us with now helps us to be prepared to take care of things that are even more valuable in the future, while we serve him on earth or in heaven.

Discussion Questions

- How could the devil try to tempt you to be dishonest about money?
- How could you resist?

Prayer Prompter

Thank you for providing for our needs. Help us to be wise, honest, and generous with money and everything else you give us.

Can't Serve Two Masters
Luke 16:13; Matthew 6:24

Memory Verse

"No servant can serve two masters. Either he will hate the one and love the other, or he will be devoted to the one and despise the other. You cannot serve both God and Money" (Luke 16:13).

Attention Grabber

Close your eyes, set a quarter against each lid, and squint to hold the quarters in place. Let the kids try to do the trick, too. Explain that if your eyes are on money all of the time, you can't see what matters more.

Living It

Everyone has to decide whether he will give most of his time and energy to getting wealthy or to serving God. If we let money become our master, we spend too much time thinking about how to get it, working for it, spending it, taking care of our possessions, and worrying about losing money. First Timothy 6:10 warns, "the love of money is a root of all kinds of evil. Some people, eager for money, have wandered from the faith and pierced themselves with many griefs." Colossians 3:5 says greed is idol worship; it's adoring and serving money rather than God.

Discussion Questions

◎ What kind of attitude should you have toward money?
◎ How should you spend your money?

Prayer Prompter

Please forgive us if we have made money in charge of us. Help us to stay devoted to you instead of money.

What Is Highly Valued

Memory Verse

The Pharisees, who loved money, heard all this and were sneering at Jesus. He said to them, "You are the ones who justify yourselves in the eyes of men, but God knows your hearts. What is highly valued among men is detestable in God's sight" (Luke 16:14, 15).

Attention Grabber

Surprise the kids by wearing ridiculous jewelry made of cash. For example, twist a few dollar bills and tape the ends together to form necklaces and bracelets. You could tape a nickel to your finger like a ring. Ask the kids if they think other people would be impressed by your jewelry and wealth. Ask what people really do to try to impress others with their money. Does God like it?

Living It

The world tends to admire rich people, even those who got rich through dishonest means, who spend all of their money on themselves, or who feel superior to others because of their wealth. Being rich may get people's praise, but it doesn't get God's.

Discussion Questions

◉ Do we shrug off what Jesus said as the Pharisees did?
◉ Do our attitudes about money match what people around us think or do they match what Jesus said?

Prayer Prompter

Please help us to have the right attitudes about money. Please help us to show that we care more about what you think than what other people think.

Rich Man, Poor Man
Luke 16:19-31

Memory Verse

"But Abraham replied, 'Son, remember that in your lifetime you received your good things, while Lazarus received bad things, but now he is comforted here and you are in agony'" (Luke 16:25).

Attention Grabber

Write a list of people in need that your family would like to help financially. Have everyone brainstorm about ways to earn the money (if necessary) and how to give it anonymously. A fun way to give money is to put the cash in a self-sealing plastic bag, place the bag in a jar full of water, and freeze it. Then make and apply a label on the jar that says, "Cold, hard cash for _____ from a family with soft, warm hearts." Leave it on a doorstep, ring the bell, and run to a spot where you can hide and watch to be sure the people pick it up.

Living It

The rich man in today's story had all the comforts his money could buy. Purple dye was expensive, so only the wealthiest people could afford clothes made of purple fabric. Unlike the man who wore purple in this story, we need to be sensitive to the needs of people around us. It's our responsibility to share what God has given us with those who have less. In Luke 6:21, 24 Jesus promised that those who hunger now will be satisfied. He also said, "Woe to you who are rich, for you have already received your comfort."

Discussion Question

◉ How do you feel when you give money to people who need it?

Prayer Prompter

Please help us to give generously to people in need. Help us to be sensitive enough to see the needs around us. Help us to find people with needs we can meet even if they're not right around us.

If Your Brother Sins

Memory Verse

"So watch yourselves. If your brother sins, rebuke him, and if he repents, forgive him" (Luke 17:3).

Attention Grabber

Beforehand, cook and drain spaghetti noodles. Act as if you're perturbed and say, "I want to give all of you thirty lashes with a wet noodle!" Then pull out a spaghetti noodle and pretend to whip them with it. For fun, you can let everyone have a noodle for whipping each other. (Serve the rest of the noodles for dinner tonight or tomorrow night.)

Living It

Ephesians 4:2 says, "Be completely humble and gentle; be patient, bearing with one another in love." When Jesus says, "Your brother," he means anyone who also believes in Jesus. We shouldn't scold people harshly when they harm us, but if what they did is serious enough that we can't simply forget about it, we need to discuss it with them. If we bury our feelings, they can turn into a grudge. Instead, it's better to gently confront people and give them a chance to apologize or at least explain. It's important to word things in a way that will help them, not make them angry. Remember, "A gentle answer turns away wrath, but a harsh word stirs up anger" (Proverbs 15:1).

Discussion Question

⊙ If someone confronted you about something you did wrong, how could he do it in a way that you would apologize and change rather than get angry?

Prayer Prompter

Please help us know how to let people know when they have wronged us without making the problem worse.

Doing Our Duty
Luke 17:7-10

Memory Verse
"So you also, when you have done everything you were told to do, should say, 'We are unworthy servants; we have only done our duty'" (Luke 17:10).

Attention Grabber
If any of your family members have been Boy Scouts or Girl Scouts, have them show their merit badges and explain what it means to do your duty. Or you can give everyone a silly certificate or an award for doing household duties. (For example, spray paint a sponge gold and give it as the Dishwasher of the Year Award.) Explain that a duty is a responsibility, a job that you do because it is expected of you.

Living It
No one should expect to get special attention for doing his duty. We need to have a humble attitude about the work that we do for God, because nothing we can do for God is worth more than what he has done for us.

Discussion Questions
◉ What are your duties around the house? At school?
◉ What are your duties for God?

Prayer Prompter
Help us to know what our duty is and to do it faithfully and humbly.

Show Gratitude
Luke 17:11-19

Memory Verse

He threw himself at Jesus' feet and thanked him—and he was a Samaritan. Jesus asked, "Were not all ten cleansed? Where are the other nine?" (Luke 17:16, 17).

Attention Grabber

Ask your kids to do various favors for you—rub your shoulders, bring you a drink, fluff your pillow. Don't thank them for anything. See if they notice. Ask, "Did I forget to say something?" Read today's story of the ten men Jesus healed. Ask them why they think nine men didn't thank Jesus and why the one did.

Living It

What is Jesus trying to teach? It's easy to take our many blessings for granted. For example, we might not give much thought to our health until we're sick. But God wants us to be grateful for what he does. We need to understand that we owe everything to him—including our gratitude.

Discussion Question

◎ What are five things you are most grateful for right now?

Prayer Prompter

Thank you for the many, many blessings you give us. Please remind us to be grateful for all you do in our lives.

As in the Days of Noah
Luke 17:26, 27

Memory Verse

"Just as it was in the days of Noah, so also will it be in the days of the Son of Man. People were eating, drinking, marrying and being given in marriage up to the day Noah entered the ark. Then the flood came and destroyed them all" (Luke 17:26, 27).

Attention Grabber

Give everyone a small cup of animal cookies. Ask, "Who got the most pairs of animals in their ark?"

Living It

In Noah's time, people went about their normal daily lives up until the flood came and washed them away. Some people won't pay any attention to what the Bible says about Jesus' return and will not even realize they're living in the last days. But others are watching for Jesus' return and are actively serving him while they wait.

Discussion Question

◉ Would you do anything differently if you were sure Jesus would return this year?

Prayer Prompter

Please help us to be ready for Jesus' return.

Keep Asking

Memory Verse
"And will not God bring about justice for his chosen ones, who cry out to him day and night? Will he keep putting them off? I tell you, he will see that they get justice, and quickly. However, when the Son of Man comes, will he find faith on the earth?" (Luke 18:7, 8).

Attention Grabber
Put pieces of duct tape or masking tape across the knees of your pants. When the kids ask about the tape, pretend that you've worn holes in the knees of your pants from praying again and again about something. Ask them if you should just give up or if you should continue trusting God to hear and answer. Read them today's story of the persistent widow.

Living It
Have you ever complained, "It's not fair!"? A lot of things aren't fair, but someday they will be. God will see that there is justice. We can't give up even when we don't get answers to our prayers immediately. God wants us to keep knocking. He assures us that if a bad judge would help someone because she kept coming to him, of course our good God will help someone who brings the same problem to him again and again.

Discussion Question
⊚ What are some reasons God might not give us what we ask for immediately?

Prayer Prompter
Please help us to be patient when you don't answer our prayers right away. Help us to trust that you will eventually.

Proud and Humble
Luke 18:9-14

Memory Verse
"For everyone who exalts himself will be humbled, and he who humbles himself will be exalted" (Luke 18:14).

Attention Grabber
Have everyone draw a caricature of himself with a huge head and a tiny body. Discuss how God doesn't want us to get a big head about our spirituality. If we think and brag about our own goodness, we are headed for a fall. If we humbly remember how much mercy we need and that our righteousness comes from Jesus, God will exalt us.

Living It
Jesus wants for us to be like him—"gentle and humble in heart" (Matthew 11:29). If we brag to other people, we aren't showing love because 1 Corinthians 13:4, 5 says that love does not boast, it is not proud and it is not self-seeking. God wants us to appreciate that our righteousness comes from him and not ourselves (Philippians 3:9).

Discussion Question
◉ Why would it be difficult for God to use a proud person to tell others about him?

Prayer Prompter
Please help us to remember that our righteousness comes from you and not ourselves. Forgive us for being boastful to you and others. Help us to be humble, Lord.

Proud and Humble

Zacchaeus in a Tree
Luke 19:1-10

Memory Verse

"For the Son of Man came to seek and to save what was lost"
(Luke 19:10).

Attention Grabber

Tell the story of Zacchaeus. Let each child make a Zacchaeus out of chenille stems or clay. Put each Zacchaeus in a different tree. When the children's friends spot a Zacchaeus, they can tell their friends the story.

Living It

Zacchaeus changed when Jesus came to his house. Immediately Zacchaeus wanted to do right things. He promised to give to the poor and to pay back money he got dishonestly. When we spend time with Jesus, he makes us want to give up our sins and do right things.

Discussion Questions

- If Jesus came to our house to dinner, what would you say to him?
- What would you change about the way you live?

Prayer Prompter

Thank you for saving us. Please remind us to spend time with you. Now that you are our Savior, please help us to follow you as our Lord.

Before the Rooster Crows

Luke 22:31-34; Mark 14:30

Memory Verse

Jesus answered, "I tell you, Peter, before the rooster crows today, you will deny three times that you know me" (Luke 22:34).

Attention Grabber

Who can do the best rooster impersonation? What is the rooster's job? (To wake up everyone.) How did the rooster wake up Peter? (It made Peter realize that Jesus' prophecy had come true—Peter had said three times he didn't know Jesus.)

Living It

If we are praying, Jesus can warn us before we sin. He can tell us how to avoid temptations that are coming. He tried to warn Peter, but Peter forgot what Jesus had said until it was too late. Peter said he didn't know Jesus because he saw people being cruel to Jesus and he was afraid they would be mean to him, too. Jesus said, "When you have turned back, strengthen your brothers" (Luke 22:32). When we sin, Jesus doesn't want us just to decide we're bad people and give up. He wants us to repent and get back to helping others. Simon Peter repented and the Lord used him to get the church off to an amazing start. After Simon Peter spoke one day, three thousand people became followers of Jesus (Acts 2:41)!

Discussion Question

How is disobeying God (falling out of God's will) like falling off a bike or a horse? (You need to get back on again! He wants you to repent; he still has plenty for you to do in his kingdom!)

Prayer Prompter

Please help us not to deny you, even if there are serious consequences. Please help us to repent quickly when we do sin.

King of the Jews

Luke 23:3; Matthew 27:11; Mark 15:2; John 19:16-22

Memory Verse

So Pilate asked Jesus, "Are you the king of the Jews?" "Yes, it is as you say," Jesus replied (Luke 23:3).

Attention Grabber

If you have roses with thorny stems or thorny vines in your yard, bend them into a crown shape and tape them together. If not, simply draw a thorny crown and a royal crown. Tell the kids that on earth Jesus didn't wear a royal crown; he wore a crown of thorns when he was crucified. Have them write "King of the Jews" on scraps of wood and tell them this was what was written on a sign nailed to his cross. (Save the thorny crown and one of the signs for the next devotion.)

Living It

Emphasize that many people in Bible times were disappointed that Jesus wasn't a king who would chase the Romans out of Israel, sit on a throne there, and rule over their country. Jesus was a different kind of king. He is not only reigning over the Jews, he is reigning over everything. Revelation 11:15 says, "The kingdom of the world has become the kingdom of our Lord and of his Christ, and he will reign for ever and ever."

Discussion Question

◉ Are you letting Jesus reign over your life?

Prayer Prompter

Please help us to obey you as our king.

Father, Forgive Them
Luke 23:34

Memory Verse
Jesus said, "Father, forgive them, for they do not know what they are doing" (Luke 23:34).

Attention Grabber
Beforehand, cut a large cross out of posterboard or tape two strips of butcher paper to a door in the shape of a cross. Tape the thorny crown and the sign from the last devotion to the cross. Read today's verse aloud. Then have the children write on slips of paper the names of persons they need to forgive, fold the slips, and tape their unforgiveness to the cross.

Living It
Jesus forgave people as they were killing him. No matter what anyone has done to us, it is not as bad as what was done to Jesus. Just as he forgave while being killed, Jesus wants us to quickly forgive everyone who has mistreated us.

Discussion Question
◉ Why do we put off forgiving people sometimes?

Prayer Prompter
Thank you for being so loving and forgiving. Please help us to quickly forgive everyone who mistreats us.

My Hands and My Feet
Luke 24:36-43

Memory Verse

"Look at my hands and my feet. It is I myself! Touch me and see; a ghost does not have flesh and bones, as you see I have" (Luke 24:39).

Attention Grabber

Have everyone trace around his hands with a marker on paper and write the verse inside the outlines.

Living It

When Mary Magdalene and other women saw an angel at the tomb who said Jesus had risen, they ran to tell the disciples. The disciples didn't believe them (Luke 24:1-11). Later Jesus appeared to the disciples himself. Jesus proved that everything he had said about himself was true.

Discussion Questions

◎ How would you have felt if you were there?
◎ What would you have done?

Prayer Prompter

Thank you for sending your Son to give his life for us, and thank you for raising him from the dead. Help us have faith that you will resurrect us, too.

You Must Be Born Again
John 3:1-7

Memory Verse
"You should not be surprised at my saying, 'You must be born again'"
(John 3:7).

Attention Grabber
Have a simple re-birthday party to celebrate new birth in Jesus. Serve cupcakes with birthday candles. If you don't have cupcakes and birthday candles, make re-birthday cards to give to people in your church who have accepted Jesus recently. If your children have questions about being born again, you may wish to look at page 268.

Living It
We have to be born two times because the first one doesn't last. Everyone's body dies sometime. To come into God's kingdom and have a spirit that lives forever with God, we need to be born a second time. When we believe that Jesus is "the way, the truth and the life" (John 14:6), he gives us eternal life, a new life that lasts forever. John 6:40 says, "Everyone who looks to the Son and believes in him shall have eternal life."

Discussion Question
◉ Why do we need to be born a second time?

Prayer Prompter
Thank you for giving eternal life to everyone who believes in your Son. Help us to appreciate this amazing gift.

The Wind Blows

Memory Verse

"The wind blows wherever it pleases. You hear its sound, but you cannot tell where it comes from or where it is going. So it is with everyone born of the Spirit" (John 3:8).

Attention Grabber

Make nut sailboats. Cut a triangular sail out of a small piece of paper. Push a toothpick in and out of the sail. Place clay inside a walnut or pecan shell. You can substitute putty or even chewed gum for the clay. Stick the toothpick into the clay. Place a pan of water outside and set the sailboats in it. Let the wind nudge them along like the Holy Spirit nudges those who are born again.

Living It

The Holy Spirit is a bit unpredictable, like the wind. We can feel him pushing us along, but we don't know exactly where he will send us. We need his power like a sailboat needs the wind.

Discussion Questions

⊚ What does it feel like when the Holy Spirit prompts you?
⊚ What has the Holy Spirit prompted you to do lately?

Prayer Prompter

Please help us to listen for the Holy Spirit and obey when he nudges us along. Thank you for the Holy Spirit and the power he gives us to accomplish what you want us to do.

Lift Up Jesus
John 3:14, 15; Numbers 21:6-9

Memory Verse
"Just as Moses lifted up the snake in the desert, so the Son of Man must be lifted up, that everyone who believes in him may have eternal life" (John 3:14, 15).

Attention Grabber
Give each family member a piece of foil to shape into a snake. If you have any beads, use these for beady eyes. Tell them the story of Moses from Numbers 21:6-9.

Living It
If people looked at the brass snake Moses made, they would live. Otherwise they would die. All we have to do is look to Jesus for our salvation, and we will live forever with him in heaven. Those who refuse will not. We need to "lift Jesus up" for all to see.

Discussion Question
◉ What can you do to "lift Jesus up" for everyone around you to see?

Prayer Prompter
Thank you for showing us the way to live with you forever. Please help us to introduce others to Jesus.

God So Loved the World

Memory Verse

"For God so loved the world that he gave his one and only Son, that whoever believes in him shall not perish but have eternal life" (John 3:16).

Attention Grabber

Have the kids gather sticks, or use dowel rods, and make baseball pennants by taping or gluing a long paper triangle to each stick. Let the kids write the verse on their pennants. Mention that sometimes people at baseball games and other sporting events wave this verse because it tells people the good news about Jesus.

Living It

A lot of people have the wrong idea about God. They avoid him because they think he is mad at them and wants to punish them for their sins. Actually God wants to forgive people's sins and make them happy! He loves the world so much that he let his Son give his life so that people could be saved from the punishment they deserve for sin. Whoever believes in Jesus as Savior and Lord will live forever with God.

Discussion Questions

◎ Who do you know who needs to hear this verse?
◎ Can you recite it to that person?

Prayer Prompter

Please help us to trust Jesus as our Savior and follow him as Lord. If we should recite this verse for people we know, please give us the courage to do that, and help us to be able to explain the verse.

Jesus, the Life Saver
John 3:17

Memory Verse
"For God did not send his Son into the world to condemn the world, but to save the world through him" (John 3:17).

Attention Grabber
Let each family member knot a 24-inch piece of string and loop it through a white Lifesaver hard candy to make a necklace. Explain that everyone is drowning in sin and the only way he can live forever is to ask Jesus to rescue him and be his life Savior. If you would like, let the kids make extra necklaces. When friends ask about the necklaces they're wearing, they can quote today's verse, explain it, and give their friends a Lifesaver hard candy necklace of their own.

Living It
God doesn't want to punish sin. He wants to take our sins away. He sent Jesus to rescue us from the punishment we deserve for what we've done wrong. We need him to be our life saver. Whoever believes in him will be saved from sins and given eternal life, life with God that lasts forever.

Discussion Question
◎ Why, according to this verse, did God send his Son?

Prayer Prompter
Thank you for wanting to save the world through your Son. Help the world to accept Jesus as Savior.

Never Thirst

Memory Verse

Jesus answered, "Everyone who drinks this water will be thirsty again, but whoever drinks the water I give him will never thirst. Indeed, the water I give him will become in him a spring of water welling up to eternal life" (John 4:13, 14).

Attention Grabber

Have the kids write the verse on a note card and attach it to a large water bottle or drinking cup with clear packaging tape. Tell them that it's good to drink lots of water every day. Encourage them to practice reciting the verse each time they drink water throughout the day.

Living It

Everyone is thirsty for the love, forgiveness, and peace that knowing Jesus gives. Some people search for those things all of their lives. They try to use money, or people, or even alcohol and drugs to fill those needs. Some people never realize that what they really need is Jesus.

Discussion Question

◎ How is needing Jesus like being thirsty?

Prayer Prompter

Thank you for quenching our thirsty spirits. Please help us to see how to share your living water with others.

Scriptures Tell of Jesus

John 5:39

Memory Verse

"You diligently study the Scriptures because you think that by them you possess eternal life. These are the Scriptures that testify about me" (John 5:39).

Attention Grabber

Let each family member make a bookmark for his or her Bible by writing today's verse on a strip of colored paper. The kids can decorate the bookmarks with stickers and drawings. Let them cut the edges with decorative scissors. Seal the bookmarks between pieces of Con-Tact self-adhesive cover if you have some.

Living It

The whole Bible, not just the New Testament, tells about Jesus. Whenever prophets in the Old Testament told about the Messiah, they were talking about Jesus. Many of the events in the Old Testament foreshadowed what would happen later; they showed what would happen to Jesus. For example, Jonah was in the great fish for three days and Jesus was in the tomb for three days. Manna was like Jesus, who is the bread of life. Some people didn't believe Jesus, even though he fulfilled the Old Testament prophecies. He told them their knowledge of the Scriptures didn't help them because they didn't see the truth.

Discussion Questions

- Can you name the books of the Bible?
- Have you ever hunted for something (such as Easter eggs) and been surprised that you overlooked something that was right under your nose? Many people read Scripture and overlook what is most important.

Prayer Prompter

Please help us to learn all the Bible teaches about your Son.

Scriptures Tell of Jesus

The Work Is to Believe

John 6:22-29

Memory Verse

Jesus answered, "The work of God is this: to believe in the one he has sent" (John 6:29).

Attention Grabber

Cut a diamond-shaped sign out of yellow paper. Write "Family at Work" on it. On the reverse side, write the memory verse in large letters. Cut the words apart, and have the family work together to put the verse into the correct order. Tape the words in place and flip it over so they can see the sign. If you would like, punch a hole near the top of the sign and hang it by a thread from a ceiling fan pull, doorknob, or light fixture.

Living It

Many people have the misunderstanding that if they do enough good deeds, they can earn their way to heaven. Actually, we could never do enough good to deserve living with God. When people asked what work was required, Jesus said it was to believe in him. The good things we do are fruit that show we love Jesus and are grateful that he has enabled us to go to heaven.

Discussion Question

Ⓠ Have you ever trusted your own goodness to get you to heaven? Why would that be wrong?

Prayer Prompter

Please keep our faith in your Son strong. Help us to trust Jesus and not ourselves to save us.

The Bread of Life
John 6:30-35

Memory Verse

Then Jesus declared, "I am the bread of life. He who comes to me will never go hungry, and he who believes in me will never be thirsty" *(John 6:35).*

Attention Grabber

Let the kids write "Jesus is the bread of life" on bread with cheese that can be squeezed from a can or with toothpicks dipped in food coloring that is mixed with a couple drops of milk.

Living It

Manna was bread God sent from heaven to feed the Israelites (see Exodus 16:4, 5). Jesus is like manna in many ways. Both came from heaven. Both were sent by God. People collected manna every day; we need to spend time with Jesus every day. Manna stopped their physical hunger; Jesus stops our spiritual hunger. Manna gave the people physical life; Jesus gives eternal life.

Discussion Questions

◉ What did Jesus say about bread in the Model Prayer (Matthew 6:9-13)?
◉ What does the bread of Communion represent?

Prayer Prompter

Thank you for sending the bread of life. Help us to come to you daily so our spirits don't get hungry.

The Bread of Life

Believers Will Be Raised

Memory Verse

"For my Father's will is that everyone who looks to the Son and believes in him shall have eternal life, and I will raise him up at the last day" (John 6:40).

Attention Grabber

Have the kids make a balloon model of themselves to remind them that Jesus will raise them up. They can put their feet together and trace around them onto a piece of poster board. Then they cut out the pair of feet and poke a hole in the center. After that, have them draw a self-portrait on an inflated balloon and poke the knotted end of the balloon through the hole.

Living It

Everyone who believes in Jesus will rise up to meet him when he returns. First Thessalonians 4:17, 18 says, "We who are still alive and are left will be caught up together with them in the clouds to meet the Lord in the air. And so we will be with the Lord forever. Therefore encourage each other with these words."

Discussion Question

◉ What do you think it will feel like to rise up to meet Jesus in the air?

Prayer Prompter

Thank you for wanting us to be in heaven with you. Help us to share your good news with others so they can believe and rise up to meet Jesus with us.

The Light of the World
John 8:12

Memory Verse
When Jesus spoke again to the people, he said, "I am the light of the world. Whoever follows me will never walk in darkness, but will have the light of life" (John 8:12).

Attention Grabber
Beforehand, use the pattern on page 263 and cut out a light switch plate cover for each family member. Have them write the verse on plate covers, decorate them, and then tape them over light switch plates in their bedrooms.

Living It
Light is a symbol of goodness, and darkness is a symbol of evil. In heaven there's no need for the sun or moon because of the glory of God and Jesus (Revelation 21:23). If Jesus is our Lord, we want to stay out of the darkness.

Discussion Questions
- What are some good things light does?
- How is being in sin like being in darkness? (It's hard to find your way out of it. You get hurt. It's lonely.)

Prayer Prompter
Please help us to follow Jesus and walk in the light.

Before Abraham, I Am

John 8:58

Memory Verse

"I tell you the truth," Jesus answered, *"before Abraham was born, I am!" (John 8:58).*

Attention Grabber

Before you read today's verse, give the kids eight toothpicks and tell them to arrange them to spell one of the names Jesus called himself. Hints: the name is two words, three letters, and is a name God told Moses to call him. (I AM.)

Living It

When Moses asked God what he should tell the people God's name was, God said to tell them "I AM has sent me to you" (Exodus 3:14). So when Jesus said, "Before Abraham was born, I am," he was saying that he was God and he is God. Another name for Jesus is Immanuel, which means "God with us" (Matthew 1:23). John calls Jesus the Word and says, "In the beginning was the Word, and the Word was with God, and the Word was God" (John 1:1).

Discussion Question

◉ Why do you think God called himself I AM? (Because he has always existed and always will exist.)

Prayer Prompter

We praise you, God the Father, and we praise Jesus, God the Son, and God the Holy Spirit. Help us learn more about the Father, the Son, and the Holy Spirit.

His Sheep Know His Voice
John 10:1-10

Memory Verse

"The watchman opens the gate for him, and the sheep listen to his voice. He calls his own sheep by name and leads them out. When he has brought out all his own, he goes on ahead of them, and his sheep follow him because they know his voice" (John 10:3, 4).

Attention Grabber

Secretly phone a friend whom your family knows well and ask the person to call back without identifying himself or herself. Can the kids guess who it is? Emphasize that if we know someone well, we recognize that person's voice.

Living It

Jesus wants us to know him well enough that when his Holy Spirit speaks to us, we recognize his voice. He may not speak with a voice our ears can hear, but he will speak to our spirit if we are listening. Hebrews 3:15 says, "If you hear his voice, do not harden your hearts." It's important to be able to hear him so that we can follow him. An important part of prayer is listening.

Discussion Questions

- Why can't we just put off listening to God until we have important decisions to make?
- Have you listened to him today?

Prayer Prompter

Please help us listen so we can follow Jesus.

Memory Verse

"I am the gate; whoever enters through me will be saved. He will come in and go out, and find pasture" (John 10:9).

Attention Grabber

Have a family member lie down in front of a doorway and say, "I'm the gate of the sheep pen. Are you a sheep, a goat, a robber, a wolf, or a lion?" The gate should let the kids enter only when they say they are sheep.

Living It

In Bible times, a shepherd would often lie down and sleep in the opening of the pen to protect the sheep from robbers and wild animals. In that way, the shepherd was like a gate. Who can remember Matthew 7:14, which we memorized earlier (Narrow Gate, page 73)? It says, "Small is the gate and narrow the road that leads to life, and only a few find it." Unfortunately, few people will find Jesus. Many try to get into heaven other ways, but Jesus is the only way to the Father (John 14:6).

Discussion Questions

- What wild animal are you protected from by the gate? (First Peter 5:8 says "the devil prowls around like a roaring lion looking for someone to devour.")
- In what other ways do people try to come to God other than through Jesus?

Prayer Prompter

Thank you for providing the way for us to come to you. Help us to trust Jesus to protect us from the devil.

The Good Shepherd

John 10:14, 15

Memory Verse

"I am the good shepherd; I know my sheep and my sheep know me—just as the Father knows me and I know the Father—and I lay down my life for the sheep" (John 10:14, 15).

Attention Grabber

Make shepherd's staff breadsticks. Let the kids shape refrigerated breadstick dough into ropes and then bend over the tops. Bake according to the package directions. Or if you are reading this devotion when candy canes are available, give one to each of the kids and explain that they are shaped like shepherds' staffs and remind us of the Good Shepherd.

Living It

A shepherd will risk his life for his sheep. If a robber tries to steal them or an animal tries to attack them, the shepherd will protect them. Jesus laid down his life for us by dying on the cross. He died to take the punishment for our sins so that we could live forever in heaven.

Discussion Question

◉ How can you get to know Jesus better?

Prayer Prompter

Thank you for sending your Son to be our shepherd. Help us to know him well.

No One Can Snatch Them

Memory Verse

"I give them eternal life, and they shall never perish; no one can snatch them out of my hand. My Father, who has given them to me, is greater than all; no one can snatch them out of my Father's hand" (John 10:28, 29).

Attention Grabber

Put small objects in your hand (such as jacks, candy pieces, coins, or carrot slices). Open and close your hand, letting the kids try to snatch the objects out of it. Don't let them succeed. When they give up, let them have the objects, if they are treats. (Note: Only play this game with children who are old enough that they won't put small objects other than food in their mouths.)

Living It

When we accept God's gift of eternal life through faith in Jesus, it is as if we are in God's hand. He won't let the devil snatch us away from him. You don't need to worry about anyone else taking you away from God.

Discussion Question

◉ What does it mean to be in good hands?

Prayer Prompter

Thank you for giving believers eternal life and protecting us from the enemy. Help us to trust you to protect us and keep us with you forever.

I and the Father Are One

John 10:30

Memory Verse

"I and the Father are one" (John 10:30).

Attention Grabber

Boil water. Have the kids compare the steam from the boiling water with ice and with water at room temperature. Emphasize that they each have a different name and different form, but they are all water.

Living It

The Father, the Son, and the Holy Spirit are all God. They are the same in purpose, will, love, power, perfection, glory, and goodness. They are united in their desire for people to be able to go to heaven.

Discussion Question

◉ Do you feel the love of the Father, the Son, and the Holy Spirit?

Prayer Prompter

Thank you for loving us. Please help us to grow in our understanding of you, your Son, and the Holy Spirit.

Resurrection and Life

Memory Verse

Jesus said to her, "I am the resurrection and the life. He who believes in me will live, even though he dies" (John 11:25).

Attention Grabber

Blow bubbles outdoors and emphasize that they are rising just as we will rise up to heaven someday because of Jesus. If you don't have store-bought bubbles, make a wand by simply pushing the bottom out of a paper cup. Fill a second paper cup about 1/4 full of liquid dish washing detergent. Dip the bottomless cup into the detergent and blow through the bottomless cup.

Living It

The idea of dying doesn't need to be frightening for believers. Even though our bodies will die someday, our spirits will go to live forever with God because of Jesus.

Discussion Question

◎ Does death sound frightening to you? Why or why not?

Prayer Prompter

Please keep our faith strong that we will live again because of Jesus.

A Kernel of Wheat
John 12:24

Memory Verse
"I tell you the truth, unless a kernel of wheat falls to the ground and dies, it remains only a single seed. But if it does, it produces many seeds" (John 12:24).

Attention Grabber
Pour puffed wheat cereal into a bowl. Explain that these are puffed kernels of wheat that have been sweetened. Hold a kernel in your hand. Explain that all of the kernels in the bowl could have come from a single kernel that went into the ground and produced a stalk of wheat with many kernels on it.

Living It
Just like a kernel of wheat needs to go into the ground for more wheat to live, Jesus needed to die so he could be resurrected, and we could live again also.

Discussion Questions
- Can you remember the parable Jesus told about wheat that we learned earlier (page 102)?
- What other things have to die or disappear to create new life? (caterpillars/butterflies, bulbs/flowers).

Prayer Prompter
We're grateful for the great sacrifice Jesus made for us and others. Please give us a willing attitude about the small sacrifices you ask us to make for others.

A Kernel of Wheat

The One Who Sent Me
John 12:45

Memory Verse
"When he looks at me, he sees the one who sent me" (John 12:45).

Attention Grabber
Discuss the similarities of the kids to other family members. Whose nose do they have? Whose eyes? Do they have similar personalities and dispositions to other family members?

Living It
Children resemble their parents in how they look. Jesus resembles God in who he is. He has the same qualities as his Father. Both are God. As we try to understand who God is, we can look at Jesus' life to help us. Jesus was merciful, loving, powerful, and compassionate. God the Father is, too!

Discussion Question
◉ What are some things Jesus did that help us see what God the Father is like?

Prayer Prompter
Please help us to become more like you the way that Jesus is.

Wash One Another's Feet
John 13:1-15

Memory Verse
"Now that I, your Lord and Teacher, have washed your feet, you also should wash one another's feet. I have set you an example that you should do as I have done for you" (John 13:14, 15).

Attention Grabber
Bring in a pan of soapy water and wash the kids' feet or rub them with lotion while someone reads John 13:1-15. Dry their feet. If you would like, have them trace around each other's feet onto paper and then write inside the outline something they will do to help that family member.

Living It
Washing someone's feet is a humbling experience. If the Son of God didn't think this kind of service was beneath him, we shouldn't either. Jesus was showing us that we should be willing to do anything to help others.

Discussion Questions
- What help do each of you need?
- Who will do those things for each other?

Prayer Prompter
Please help us to be willing to serve others humbly the way your Son did.

Know and Do

Memory Verse

"Now that you know these things, you will be blessed if you do them"
(John 13:17).

Attention Grabber

Let everyone make blessing booklets in which they can record ways that God has blessed their obedience. Cut sheets of paper into quarters and staple them together. Let the kids decorate the covers with stickers or drawings.

Living It

It's not enough to know what's right; we need to do what's right. The Bible says, "But be ye doers of the word, and not hearers only, deceiving your own selves" (James 1:22, *King James Version*). Some people call this "putting feet on your faith." God gives us commands because keeping them will help us and those around us.

Discussion Questions

- How could keeping each of the Ten Commandments help you and others?
- How could breaking them hurt you and others?

Prayer Prompter

Please help us to do what you want. Thank you for blessing us for following you.

Love One Another
John 13:34

Memory Verse

"A new command I give you: Love one another. As I have loved you, so you must love one another" (John 13:34).

Attention Grabber

Have family members form the letters of the word L-O-V-E with their bodies and take instant photographs. Or form hearts by dipping miniature pretzels in melted white or semisweet chocolate chips and letting the hearts cool on wax paper. Or write the verse on paper and surround it with stamped hearts. Create the stamps by cutting a sponge into small hearts and dipping them in paint.

Living It

Jesus doesn't want us to let the people around us stay strangers. He wants us to love them. Instead of treating people as they have treated us, Jesus wants us to treat them the way *he* has treated us. We know Jesus loves us because the Bible tells us he does, but we also know because he forgives us, because he takes care of us, because he listens to us, because he is always kind to us. Those are all ways we can treat other people to show our love for them.

Discussion Questions

◉ Do the people that you love know it?
◉ How can you show them?

Prayer Prompter

Please help us to love others as you have loved us. Help us know how to show that love for them.

You Are My Disciples

Memory Verse

"By this all men will know that you are my disciples, if you love one another" (John 13:35).

Attention Grabber

Have each kid make a gift by wrapping one end of a sparkly chenille stem around the eraser end of a pencil and then shaping the other end of the chenille stem into a heart or star shape. The kids can show love by giving away the gifts they've made.

Living It

When people are trying to find a church where people follow Jesus, they will look for one where the people show love. Love is the main thing Jesus emphasized. People will know we love Jesus if we love them and each other. When people see that believers are more loving than most people, they want to know how we are so full of love. Then we can tell them about how Jesus fills us with love for others.

Discussion Questions

◉ What are three ways people have shown love to you this week?

◉ Who can you show love to those same ways?

Prayer Prompter

Please help us live your command to love others. Help others to know we're your disciples.

Don't Be Troubled

John 14:1

Memory Verse

"Do not let your hearts be troubled. Trust in God; trust also in me"
(John 14:1).

Attention Grabber

Fill a bowl with water. Add a couple drops of red food coloring. Let one of the kids stir the color into the water. Explain that this bowl is like your heart. When water is troubled, it is disturbed and it isn't calm. Hearts are the same way. Stir the water to show how we feel sometimes when problems come. Or if you live near water, teach the kids to skip a rock and point out the troubled water where the rock touches it and causes ripples.

Living It

This is a very comforting verse in times of trouble. We have control over whether our hearts are troubled or not. Jesus explains how we can keep them calm: by trusting in God and in Jesus. We can trust that "in all things God works for the good of those who love him, who have been called according to his purpose" (Romans 8:28). We can trust that Jesus gives us eternal life because we believe in him (1 John 5:11). That will calm the ripples trouble causes in our hearts.

Discussion Question

◉ Can you think of something that happened to you, which seemed bad at the time but later God turned it into something good?

Prayer Prompter

Thank you for making things work out for our good. Help us to trust you and your Son always. Thank you for the peace you give us.

Preparing a Place for You
John 14:2-4

Memory Verse

"In my Father's house are many rooms; if it were not so, I would have told you. I am going there to prepare a place for you." (John 14:2).

Attention Grabber

Draw a floor plan of the place where you live on a poster board and let the kids draw the furniture in their rooms.

Living It

Just as there is a place for every family member in our home, everyone who has become part of the family of God by trusting in Jesus has a place in heaven. We don't know a lot about heaven, so we can't draw a floor plan of the houses or a map of the city, but we can be sure that it is a real place. Jesus has gone there to get everything ready for us. When he returns, he will take us there.

Discussion Question

- What do you look forward to about heaven? (things such as worshiping God, seeing loved ones, no crying, no sickness, no death)

Prayer Prompter

It makes us happy to think of praising you in heaven. We're very thankful that Jesus is preparing a place for us in your house. Thanks for wanting us to live with you forever.

Way, Truth, Life

John 14:6

Memory Verse

"I am the way and the truth and the life. No one comes to the Father except through me" (John 14:6).

Attention Grabber

Let the kids help you make two stacks of plastic blocks, wooden blocks, or boxes. Explain that it is as if we are standing on one side and we can't get to the other side where God is because we are separated by sin. We can't jump across. Add a bridge (or ruler) that connects the two stacks and explain that God reaches out his love and forgiveness to us through Jesus. Or visit a nearby bridge and let everyone sketch the bridge as a reminder of Jesus.

Living It

Jesus connects us to God. There is no other way to get to God without trusting in Jesus to take away our sins. When we believe the truth about him, he gives us eternal life.

Discussion Questions

- Since there is only one way to heaven, why do people try other ways? What other ways do they try?
- How is Jesus like a bridge?

Prayer Prompter

Thank you for the amazing gift of eternal life through Jesus. Help us to trust him as the way, the truth, and the life. Help us to tell others about him.

If You Love Me, Obey Me

Memory Verse

"If you love me, you will obey what I command" (John 14:15).

Attention Grabber

Let a family member play "He-loves-me-he-loves-me-not," pulling petals from a flower (real or artificial). Explain that God has a better way of determining whether or not we love him.

Living It

God can tell whether we love him or not by how we obey him. If we love Jesus, we don't want to do things that make him unhappy. We trust that his commands are for our good. Loving him and feeling his love make it easier to keep his command to love other people.

Discussion Question

◉ Which of your actions show your love for God?

Prayer Prompter

Thank you for loving us. Help us to show our love for you and your Son by keeping your commands.

The Counselor
John 14:16, 17

Memory Verse
"And I will ask the Father, and he will give you another Counselor to be with you forever—the Spirit of truth. The world cannot accept him, because it neither sees him nor knows him. But you know him, for he lives with you and will be in you" (John 14:16, 17).

Attention Grabber
If you have a large shell in your home, let the kids take turns listening for the sound of the ocean in it. Or turn the volume on your stereo very low and play a song the kids know. Who can listen well enough to hear what it is? Emphasize that they had to listen very carefully to hear it.

Living It
First Corinthians 6:19 says to believers, "Your body is a temple of the Holy Spirit;" it's God's house. The Holy Spirit doesn't usually speak with a voice we can hear with our ears; we have to be listening with our spirit. John 16:13 says "he will guide you into all truth" and "will tell you what is yet to come." In Acts 8:29-40 the Spirit told Philip to go near a chariot. He obeyed and got the chance to tell a man about Jesus. Paul, whose letters make up a large part of the New Testament, made his decisions based on what the Holy Spirit told him: "And now, compelled by the Spirit, I am going to Jerusalem, not knowing what will happen to me there" (Acts 20:22). Romans 8:5 says that those who live in accordance with the Spirit have their minds set on what the Spirit desires.

Discussion Question
◉ How is your life different when you're trying to listen to the Holy Spirit and when you're not?

Prayer Prompter
Thank you for your Holy Spirit. Please help us to quiet ourselves and listen to him.

Not As Orphans
John 14:18

Memory Verse

"I will not leave you as orphans; I will come to you" (John 14:18).

Attention Grabber

If you have the videotape of the movie *Annie* or the soundtrack from it, play the chorus of "It's a Hard Knock Life." Or describe Little Orphan Annie and the way orphanages once were.

Living It

Jesus won't leave us feeling like we don't have parents, as if no one takes care of us. In Isaiah 66:13, God promises, "As a mother comforts her child, so will I comfort you." Romans 8:15, 16 says, "We received the Spirit of sonship. And by him we cry, '*Abba*, Father.' The Spirit himself testifies with our spirit that we are God's children." The word *Abba* means "Daddy" or "Papa." To call God that means that we feel affection and closeness to him.

Discussion Questions

◎ Do you let God comfort you like your mother?
◎ Do you feel the love he has for you like a father?

Prayer Prompter

Thank you for taking care of us like a parent. Help us run to you for our comfort and guidance.

He Lives So We Live
John 14:19

Memory Verse
"Because I live, you also will live" (John 14:19).

Attention Grabber
Wrap clear tape around paper clips and have each family member draw a smiley face on a paper clip to represent himself. Lift up the "paper-clip people" using a magnet, and explain that someday we will rise to heaven because Jesus did. Or if you have table-tennis balls, let the kids draw their faces on them and then place them, one at a time, above the airflow of a blow dryer that is pointed upward. The table-tennis ball will float in the air.

Living It
Because Jesus lives even though his body died, we will live even after our bodies die. The word "resurrected" means risen from the dead. Can you remember John 11:25? Jesus said, "I am the resurrection and the life. He who believes in me will live, even though he dies." Jesus has victory over death, and it has lost its sting (1 Corinthians 15:52-57). God has the power to give us new life.

Discussion Question
◎ Many people are afraid of death. Why don't believers need to fear?

Prayer Prompter
Thank you for your promise to resurrect us. Help us to trust you and not to fear death.

The Holy Spirit Reminds

Memory Verse

"But the Counselor, the Holy Spirit, whom the Father will send in my name, will teach you all things and will remind you of everything I have said to you" (John 14:26).

Attention Grabber

Tie a piece of twine or yarn around your index finger. Explain that sometimes people do that to help them remember something. Ask the kids what they do to help them remember things.

Living It

In today's verse Jesus was telling his disciples that he was going to leave them, but that the Holy Spirit would come and help them remember the things he said. If we are Christians, the Holy Spirit lives in us, too. He helps us to remember things the Lord has said to us. If we study his Word, the Bible, when we need to remember what we learned, the Holy Spirit will bring those verses to mind.

Discussion Question

⦿ How have Bible verses helped you during times of trouble or when you were telling someone about Jesus?

Prayer Prompter

Thank you for the Holy Spirit. Help us to learn from him. Please help us through him when we need to remember things Jesus has said.

My Peace I Give You
John 14:27

Memory Verse
"Peace I leave with you; my peace I give you. I do not give to you as the world gives. Do not let your hearts be troubled and do not be afraid" (John 14:27).

Attention Grabber
Place a bowl of canned peas on the table and quote or read today's verse. Ask, "Are these what he meant?" Ask the kids to explain what Jesus really meant by "peace" (unafraid, undisturbed, calm). Let them use toothpicks to connect the peas to form letters of the word "PEACE."

Living It
There are many fearful and troubled people who don't know Jesus. People in the world sometimes try to get rid of those feelings with drugs, alcohol, and other things that don't work. When we get to know Jesus and his overwhelming love for us, he gives us peace because "There is no fear in love. But perfect love drives out fear" (1 John 4:18). Romans 8:15 says, "For you did not receive a spirit that makes you a slave again to fear." Peace is one of the fruit of God's Spirit (Galatians 5:22).

Discussion Question
◉ When you start to feel afraid, how can you fight it?

Prayer Prompter
Thank you for the peace that comes from knowing your Son and trusting that you save us and protect us.

Vine and Branches
John 15:1-11

Memory Verse
"I am the vine; you are the branches. If a man remains in me and I in him, he will bear much fruit; apart from me you can do nothing" (John 15:5).

Attention Grabber
Make simple homemade grape juice. Let the kids drop seedless grapes into a self-sealing plastic freezer bag, seal the top edges of the bag (squeezing out any air), pound the grapes with their fists or step on them as people did in Bible times, and then pour the juice through a strainer into a cup. Be sure to leave some grapes on the branches for a visual aid.

Living It
Will grapes that we buy in the store keep growing when we bring them home? Why not? (They have been cut off from the vine. They can't get their strength through it anymore.) Like the grapes, our spirit stops growing if we don't stay attached to Jesus. It is only with his help and through his power that we can become the way he wants us to be and accomplish what he wants us to do. No matter how hard we try to be a good person, it is only through the Holy Spirit that we can develop "love, joy, peace, patience, kindness, goodness, faithfulness, gentleness, and self-control" (Galatians 5:22, 23). As we spend time with Jesus in prayer, he grows those virtues in us.

Discussion Questions
◎ The people we hang around influence us to be like them; how can being with Jesus influence us to be like him?
◎ What helps you to stay attached to the vine?

Prayer Prompter
Please help us to stay attached to Jesus and to keep growing.

No Greater Love
John 15:13

Memory Verse
"Greater love has no one than this, that he lay down his life for his friends" (John 15:13).

Attention Grabber
Lay a man's suit coat on the floor. Mention that gentlemen used to throw their capes or coats over puddles so ladies could cross them without ruining their shoes. Have the kids imagine that the coat represents the life Jesus laid down so we could cross over to God without sin ruining us.

Living It
Jesus laid down his life for us. He had a choice about whether to give his life or not. He said, "No one takes it from me, but I lay it down of my own accord. I have authority to lay it down and authority to take it up again" (John 10:18). Jesus laid it down because he loved us and considered us his friends. He showed the greatest love of all.

Discussion Questions
- Does it make you feel loved to think about what Jesus suffered for you?
- Do you feel that you are his friend?

Prayer Prompter
We're grateful that Jesus loved us enough to lay down his life for us. Please help us to feel that love and extend it to others.

Take Heart!

Memory Verse

"I have told you these things, so that in me you may have peace. In this world you will have trouble. But take heart! I have overcome the world" (John 16:33).

Attention Grabber

Put a rose in a vase, pour rose petal potpourri into a dish, let the kids smell rose-scented perfume, or spray rose-scented air freshener. Ask what the expression "I never promised you a rose garden" means. (No one promised you that everything in life would be rosy, beautiful, and perfect.)

Living It

Life in this world isn't always easy. We need to be careful not to let the hardships we suffer discourage us or damage our faith. First Peter 1:6-8 says that even though we have to suffer grief in all kinds of trials for a little while, these help our faith grow. We see how God comes through to help us and we trust him more. As we go through difficult experiences, it helps us take heart if we remember that Jesus has been through it all himself. Hebrews 4:15 says, "For we do not have a high priest who is unable to sympathize with our weaknesses, but we have one who has been tempted in every way, just as we are—yet was without sin." Jesus overcame all of the hardships and temptations of his life, and he will help us, too!

Discussion Question

◉ What are some trials our family has overcome with Jesus' help?

Prayer Prompter

Please help us to take heart and be overcomers. Please give us your peace and keep us strong no matter what trials and temptations we face in this life.

Take Heart!

Eternal Life
John 17:3

Memory Verse
"Now this is eternal life: that they may know you, the only true God, and Jesus Christ, whom you have sent" (John 17:3).

Attention Grabber
Beforehand, tear the cover off of a magazine, cut away the photo and tape the magazine name and subtitles over the glass frame of a large close-up photo of a family member. Ask the difference between knowing about famous people and knowing someone personally.

Living It
The only way to have everlasting life with God is to know him and his Son whom he sent. God wants us to have a relationship with him, not just know about him. The best way to get to know anyone is to spend time together. Try to spend at least fifteen minutes each time you pray so that you get past the surface issues and begin to really open up to God. Then don't rush away; spend time listening to how God feels about what you've said and what he wants you to know and do. If it helps you to stay focused, you might want to take notes as you pray about what you've said to God and what you feel that God wants you to know and do.

Discussion Question
◉ Do you feel as though you're just part of God's and Jesus' fan club, or do you feel you know them personally, too?

Prayer Prompter
Please help us to know you and your Son well.

Believe Without Seeing
John 20:29

Memory Verse

Then Jesus told him, "Because you have seen me, you have believed; blessed are those who have not seen and yet have believed" (John 20:29).

Attention Grabber

Have each family member take a turn being "It" (the person who closes her eyes). Another family member sneaks up from behind, covers It's eyes with his hands, and says "Guess who!" in a disguised voice. Emphasize that even though It can't see the person behind her, it is pretty easy for her to tell who is behind her.

Living It

We don't have to see Jesus to know who he is and to believe in him. It takes faith to believe in someone you haven't seen. We are blessed for believing, both now and forever.

Discussion Questions

- What other things do you believe in, even if you haven't seen them?
- How have you already been blessed by believing in Jesus?

Prayer Prompter

Thank you for the gift of faith you have given us to believe in Jesus even though we have never seen him. Please keep our faith strong.

Feed My Sheep
John 21:17

Memory Verse

The third time he said to him, "Simon son of John, do you love me?" Peter was hurt because Jesus asked him the third time, "Do you love me?" He said, "Lord, you know all things; you know that I love you."
Jesus said, "Feed my sheep" (John 21:17).

Attention Grabber

Put a handful of grass in a bowl and place it in front of a family member. Ask, "Is this what Jesus meant when he told Peter to feed his sheep and lambs?"

Living It

Before Jesus was arrested, he warned that Peter would deny him, and he told Peter, "When you have turned back, strengthen your brothers" (Luke 22:32). Now Peter is back with Jesus, and Jesus is saying it another way: feed my sheep. He also said to feed his lambs. What's the difference between sheep and lambs? (Lambs are young sheep.) Adults and children are all important to Jesus.

Discussion Question

◉ How can we feed Jesus' sheep and lambs?

Prayer Prompter

Please help us to know exactly how you want us to feed the sheep and lambs around us.

More Blessed to Give

Memory Verse

"In everything I did, I showed you that by this kind of hard work we must help the weak, remembering the words the Lord Jesus himself said: 'It is more blessed to give than to receive'" (Acts 20:35).

Attention Grabber

Put a large gift bow on the head of one of the kids. Ask what it means to give of yourself.

Living It

The second half of this verse is often used to emphasize that it's more fun to give gifts than receive them, which is true, but it has even more meaning. God wants us to give of ourselves—to work hard for others, giving our time, our labor, our money, our concern, and our love to those who need it.

Discussion Questions

◉ What is the most fun you have had giving to someone else?
◉ What can we give to someone else this week?

Prayer Prompter

Please help us to be generous in every way with others.

Alpha and Omega
Revelation 1:8

Memory Verse
"I am the Alpha and the Omega," says the Lord God, "who is, and who was, and who is to come, the Almighty" (Revelation 1:8).

Attention Grabber
Time how many seconds it takes the family to seat themselves on the floor in alphabetical order. Can the youngest child say his alphabet? Can anyone say the alphabet backward?

Living It
The Greek alphabet starts with a letter called "alpha" and ends with a letter called "omega." It was like Jesus was saying he is the A and the Z. Jesus was alive before he was born in Bethlehem, and he lived after his crucifixion. He is alive now, and he will be alive after the end of time. He has seen everything that has happened, and he sees everything that will happen in the future. Not only is he always there and always has been, he is all-powerful to help us.

Discussion Question
◉ Do you remember the first time you felt that Jesus was with you?

Prayer Prompter
Thank you for always being there for us.

I Stand at the Door
Revelation 3:20

Memory Verse
"Here I am! I stand at the door and knock. If anyone hears my voice and opens the door, I will come in and eat with him, and he with me" *(Revelation 3:20).*

Attention Grabber
Beforehand, have a parent or oldest child stand outside, hold a picture of Jesus from a Bible storybook in front of the peephole of the door, and knock. Lift each of the kids up to look through the peephole. If you don't have a peephole, open the door a crack and let the kids peek outside at the picture of Jesus. When the family member has come inside, let everyone listen to your heartbeat and mention that it almost sounds like knocking on a door. If you have already accepted Jesus, let them know that you have already opened your heart's door to him.

Living It
Jesus wants to come into our hearts and into our everyday lives. He doesn't force his way in; he waits for us to welcome him. He keeps waiting and knocking until we are ready to open up to him. (If this seems like a good time to ask a child about trusting Jesus, see page 268 for help.)

Discussion Question
Ⓠ Why might some people hesitate opening up to Jesus?

Prayer Prompter
Please help us to keep our hearts open to you and Jesus.

I Am Coming Soon
Revelation 22:20

Memory Verse
He who testifies to these things says, "Yes, I am coming soon." Amen. Come, Lord Jesus (Revelation 22:20).

Attention Grabber
Mention that sometimes when people return from a trip, others hang a Welcome banner for them. Have the kids make one for Jesus on butcher paper, computer printer paper, or typing paper taped together. You can hang it whenever you have overnight guests or when a family member returns from a trip, remembering that you are also waiting for Jesus to return.

Living It
It might seem like a long time since Jesus said he was coming soon, but to the Lord a thousand years are like a day (2 Peter 3:8). He is patient about returning because he wants everyone to have a chance to repent first (2 Peter 3:9). We need to tell others about him so they can be ready, and we need to do what Jesus said in Mark 13:37: "What I say to you, I say to everyone: 'Watch!'"

Discussion Questions
- How are you serving Jesus as you watch and wait for his return?
- What will you be happy about when he comes?

Prayer Prompter
Please show us what you want us to do to help others learn about Jesus so they'll be ready for his return. Please soften the hearts of our family and friends who haven't accepted Jesus yet. Help us to remain watchful and ready ourselves for that great day when Jesus returns. Come, Lord Jesus!

I Am Coming Soon

Optional Supplies

Most of the devotions use items you probably already have. If you don't happen to have the needed materials, don't worry. There is usually a simple alternate activity. If you would like to plan ahead to be sure you have everything, please make yourself a shopping list by circling the items you need to buy. If a devotion isn't listed, no materials are needed for it.

page 17   slices of bread
page 19   chairs
page 21   pens and white Con-Tact self-adhesive cover or paper
page 23   comforter
page 24   large safety pin, towel
page 25   salty snack, cold drinks
page 27   masking tape, peanut butter, window cleaner, paper towels
page 28   coin
page 30   boiled eggs, popcorn, or another snack you usually salt (unsalted)
page 31   glow-in-the-dark object (such as a clock, wristwatch, or toy)
page 32   votive candle, match, and bowl; or a birthday candle, match, and ceramic mug
page 33   inexpensive flashlights with batteries
page 34   magazines with several illustrations of items you actually have and the items (such as a picture of a banana and an actual banana)
page 37   stuffed or bean-filled animal (preferably a lamb or a bull)
page 38   can of soda
page 39   cup of water, cinnamon, cloves, saucepan
page 40   long-sleeved, oversized shirt
page 41   wedding and anniversary pictures of a happily married couple
page 43   paper towel and blush or lipstick
page 44   nightgown and robe resembling Bible times attire
page 45   time for a two-mile walk; or a broom and music
page 46   food to go in a bag of groceries for a food pantry or a plate of sandwiches for the homeless
page 48   clay; or item made out of clay (if homemade bread clay—white bread, school glue, water; see recipe on page 265)
page 49   star stickers, lamp that can shine like a spotlight
page 50   toy trumpet or kazoo (if homemade—toilet paper roll, wax paper, rubber band, pencil; see directions on page 264), cup, coin
page 51   pen
page 52   paper plate, scissors, Bibles
page 54   lyrics to worship song such as "Holy, Holy, Holy"
page 55   paper, pens
page 56   paper plates, hot bread
page 57   paper, pen
page 58   fishing lures
page 59   kneadable erasers or plain erasers, pencils, paper
page 61   catalog
page 62   obituary from the newspaper
page 63   posterboard or other large paper, ink pad or red paper, paste
page 64   milk carton, white spray paint, scissors, twine, nail, stapler, twig
page 66   blades of grass; or fresh wildflowers (if available), wax paper, large book
page 67   small snack and doll outfit or sock

Know-It-By-Heart

Chart for _____

❑ Mt. 4:4	❑ Mt. 6:27	❑ Mt. 15:32	❑ Mk. 1:41	❑ Lk. 19:10
❑ Mt. 4:7	❑ Mt. 6:28, 29	❑ Mt. 16:3	❑ Mk. 2:14	❑ Lk. 22:34
❑ Mt. 4:10	❑ Mt. 6:33	❑ Mt. 16:15, 16	❑ Mk. 5:19	❑ Lk. 23:3
❑ Mt. 4:17	❑ Mt. 6:34	❑ Mt. 16:24	❑ Mk. 5:36	❑ Lk. 23:34
❑ Mt. 4:19	❑ Mt. 7:3	❑ Mt. 16:25	❑ Mk. 6:49, 50	❑ Lk. 24:39
❑ Mt. 5:3	❑ Mt. 7:6	❑ Mt. 16:26	❑ Mk. 7:6, 7	❑ Jn. 3:7
❑ Mt. 5:4	❑ Mt. 7:7, 8	❑ Mt. 16:27	❑ Mk. 7:21-23	❑ Jn. 3:8
❑ Mt. 5:5	❑ Mt. 7:9-11	❑ Mt. 17:20, 21	❑ Mk. 9:31	❑ Jn. 3:14, 15
❑ Mt. 5:6	❑ Mt. 7:13, 14	❑ Mt. 18:3	❑ Mk. 9:35	❑ Jn. 3:16
❑ Mt. 5:7	❑ Mt. 7:15, 16	❑ Mt. 18:4	❑ Mk. 11:24	❑ Jn. 3:17
❑ Mt. 5:8	❑ Mt. 7:21	❑ Mt. 18:5	❑ Mk. 12:43, 44	❑ Jn. 4:13, 14
❑ Mt. 5:9	❑ Mt. 7:24	❑ Mt. 18:6	❑ Mk. 14:36	❑ Jn. 5:39
❑ Mt. 5:10	❑ Mt. 8:26	❑ Mt. 18:10	❑ Mk. 16:15, 16	❑ Jn. 6:29
❑ Mt. 5:13	❑ Mt. 9:6	❑ Mt. 18:12	❑ Mk. 16:17	❑ Jn. 6:35
❑ Mt. 5:14	❑ Mt. 9:12	❑ Mt. 18:15	❑ Lk. 6:27, 28	❑ Jn. 6:40
❑ Mt. 5:15	❑ Mt. 9:29	❑ Mt. 18:19	❑ Lk. 6:31	❑ Jn. 8:12
❑ Mt. 5:16	❑ Mt. 9:37, 38	❑ Mt. 18:20	❑ Lk. 6:37	❑ Jn. 8:58
❑ Mt. 5:17	❑ Mt. 10:7, 8	❑ Mt. 18:21, 22	❑ Lk. 6:38	❑ Jn. 10:3, 4
❑ Mt. 5:20	❑ Mt. 10:16	❑ Mt. 18:32, 33	❑ Lk. 7:47	❑ Jn. 10:9
❑ Mt. 5:22	❑ Mt. 10:28	❑ Mt. 19:6	❑ Lk. 9:58	❑ Jn. 10:14, 15
❑ Mt. 5:23, 24	❑ Mt. 10:30	❑ Mt. 19:14	❑ Lk. 9:62	❑ Jn. 10:28, 29
❑ Mt. 5:25	❑ Mt. 10:31	❑ Mt. 19:24-26	❑ Lk. 10:41, 42	❑ Jn. 10:30
❑ Mt. 5:27, 28	❑ Mt. 10:32, 33	❑ Mt. 19:29	❑ Lk. 11:34, 35	❑ Jn. 11:25
❑ Mt. 5:30	❑ Mt. 10:37	❑ Mt. 20:14, 15	❑ Lk. 11:42	❑ Jn. 12:24
❑ Mt. 5:32	❑ Mt. 10:42	❑ Mt. 20:28	❑ Lk. 11:46	❑ Jn. 12:45
❑ Mt. 5:36, 37	❑ Mt. 11:4, 5	❑ Mt. 22:14	❑ Lk. 12:1	❑ Jn. 13:14, 15
❑ Mt. 5:39	❑ Mt. 11:19	❑ Mt. 22:21	❑ Lk. 12:2, 3	❑ Jn. 13:17
❑ Mt. 5:40	❑ Mt. 11:25	❑ Mt. 22:29	❑ Lk. 12:11, 12	❑ Jn. 13:34
❑ Mt. 5:41	❑ Mt. 11:28	❑ Mt. 22:37, 38	❑ Lk. 12:15	❑ Jn. 13:35
❑ Mt. 5:42	❑ Mt. 11:29	❑ Mt. 22:39	❑ Lk. 12:20, 21	❑ Jn. 14:1
❑ Mt. 5:46, 47	❑ Mt. 11:30	❑ Mt. 22:40	❑ Lk. 12:32-34	❑ Jn. 14:2
❑ Mt. 5:48	❑ Mt. 12:11, 12	❑ Mt. 23:3	❑ Lk. 12:40	❑ Jn. 14:6
❑ Mt. 6:1	❑ Mt. 12:25	❑ Mt. 23:24	❑ Lk. 13:4, 5	❑ Jn. 14:15
❑ Mt. 6:2	❑ Mt. 12:30	❑ Mt. 23:25, 26	❑ Lk. 14:8	❑ Jn. 14:16, 17
❑ Mt. 6:3, 4	❑ Mt. 12:36	❑ Mt. 23:28	❑ Lk. 14:13, 14	❑ Jn. 14:18
❑ Mt. 6:6	❑ Mt. 12:40	❑ Mt. 23:37	❑ Lk. 14:28	❑ Jn. 14:19
❑ Mt. 6:7, 8	❑ Mt. 13:23	❑ Mt. 24:14	❑ Lk. 15:8	❑ Jn. 14:26
❑ Mt. 6:9	❑ Mt. 13:24, 25	❑ Mt. 24:27	❑ Lk. 15:20	❑ Jn. 14:27
❑ Mt. 6:10	❑ Mt. 13:31, 32	❑ Mt. 24:30, 31	❑ Lk. 16:10, 11	❑ Jn. 15:5
❑ Mt. 6:11	❑ Mt. 13:33	❑ Mt. 24:36	❑ Lk. 16:13	❑ Jn. 15:13
❑ Mt. 6:12	❑ Mt. 13:45, 46	❑ Mt. 25:13	❑ Lk. 16:14, 15	❑ Jn. 16:33
❑ Mt. 6:13	❑ Mt. 13:47	❑ Mt. 25:21	❑ Lk. 16:25	❑ Jn. 17:3
❑ Mt. 6:14, 15	❑ Mt. 13:52	❑ Mt. 25:40	❑ Lk. 17:3	❑ Jn. 20:29
❑ Mt. 6:17	❑ Mt. 13:57	❑ Mt. 26:26-28	❑ Lk. 17:10	❑ Jn. 21:17
❑ Mt. 6:19	❑ Mt. 15:3	❑ Mt. 26:41	❑ Lk. 17:16, 17	❑ Acts 20:35
❑ Mt. 6:20	❑ Mt. 15:5, 6	❑ Mt. 26:53, 54	❑ Lk. 17:26, 27	❑ Rev. 1:8
❑ Mt. 6:21	❑ Mt. 15:11	❑ Mt. 28:19, 20	❑ Lk. 18:7, 8	❑ Rev. 3:20
❑ Mt. 6:25, 26	❑ Mt. 15:14	❑ Mt. 28:20	❑ Lk. 18:14	❑ Rev. 22:20

Know-It-By-Heart

Chart for _____

❑ Mt. 4:4	❑ Mt. 6:27	❑ Mt. 15:32	❑ Mk. 1:41	❑ Lk. 19:10
❑ Mt. 4:7	❑ Mt. 6:28, 29	❑ Mt. 16:3	❑ Mk. 2:14	❑ Lk. 22:34
❑ Mt. 4:10	❑ Mt. 6:33	❑ Mt. 16:15, 16	❑ Mk. 5:19	❑ Lk. 23:3
❑ Mt. 4:17	❑ Mt. 6:34	❑ Mt. 16:24	❑ Mk. 5:36	❑ Lk. 23:34
❑ Mt. 4:19	❑ Mt. 7:3	❑ Mt. 16:25	❑ Mk. 6:49, 50	❑ Lk. 24:39
❑ Mt. 5:3	❑ Mt. 7:6	❑ Mt. 16:26	❑ Mk. 7:6, 7	❑ Jn. 3:7
❑ Mt. 5:4	❑ Mt. 7:7, 8	❑ Mt. 16:27	❑ Mk. 7:21-23	❑ Jn. 3:8
❑ Mt. 5:5	❑ Mt. 7:9-11	❑ Mt. 17:20, 21	❑ Mk. 9:31	❑ Jn. 3:14, 15
❑ Mt. 5:6	❑ Mt. 7:13, 14	❑ Mt. 18:3	❑ Mk. 9:35	❑ Jn. 3:16
❑ Mt. 5:7	❑ Mt. 7:15, 16	❑ Mt. 18:4	❑ Mk. 11:24	❑ Jn. 3:17
❑ Mt. 5:8	❑ Mt. 7:21	❑ Mt. 18:5	❑ Mk. 12:43, 44	❑ Jn. 4:13, 14
❑ Mt. 5:9	❑ Mt. 7:24	❑ Mt. 18:6	❑ Mk. 14:36	❑ Jn. 5:39
❑ Mt. 5:10	❑ Mt. 8:26	❑ Mt. 18:10	❑ Mk. 16:15, 16	❑ Jn. 6:29
❑ Mt. 5:13	❑ Mt. 9:6	❑ Mt. 18:12	❑ Mk. 16:17	❑ Jn. 6:35
❑ Mt. 5:14	❑ Mt. 9:12	❑ Mt. 18:15	❑ Lk. 6:27, 28	❑ Jn. 6:40
❑ Mt. 5:15	❑ Mt. 9:29	❑ Mt. 18:19	❑ Lk. 6:31	❑ Jn. 8:12
❑ Mt. 5:16	❑ Mt. 9:37, 38	❑ Mt. 18:20	❑ Lk. 6:37	❑ Jn. 8:58
❑ Mt. 5:17	❑ Mt. 10:7, 8	❑ Mt. 18:21, 22	❑ Lk. 6:38	❑ Jn. 10:3, 4
❑ Mt. 5:20	❑ Mt. 10:16	❑ Mt. 18:32, 33	❑ Lk. 7:47	❑ Jn. 10:9
❑ Mt. 5:22	❑ Mt. 10:28	❑ Mt. 19:6	❑ Lk. 9:58	❑ Jn. 10:14, 15
❑ Mt. 5:23, 24	❑ Mt. 10:30	❑ Mt. 19:14	❑ Lk. 9:62	❑ Jn. 10:28, 29
❑ Mt. 5:25	❑ Mt. 10:31	❑ Mt. 19:24-26	❑ Lk. 10:41, 42	❑ Jn. 10:30
❑ Mt. 5:27, 28	❑ Mt. 10:32, 33	❑ Mt. 19:29	❑ Lk. 11:34, 35	❑ Jn. 11:25
❑ Mt. 5:30	❑ Mt. 10:37	❑ Mt. 20:14, 15	❑ Lk. 11:42	❑ Jn. 12:24
❑ Mt. 5:32	❑ Mt. 10:42	❑ Mt. 20:28	❑ Lk. 11:46	❑ Jn. 12:45
❑ Mt. 5:36, 37	❑ Mt. 11:4, 5	❑ Mt. 22:14	❑ Lk. 12:1	❑ Jn. 13:14, 15
❑ Mt. 5:39	❑ Mt. 11:19	❑ Mt. 22:21	❑ Lk. 12:2, 3	❑ Jn. 13:17
❑ Mt. 5:40	❑ Mt. 11:25	❑ Mt. 22:29	❑ Lk. 12:11, 12	❑ Jn. 13:34
❑ Mt. 5:41	❑ Mt. 11:28	❑ Mt. 22:37, 38	❑ Lk. 12:15	❑ Jn. 13:35
❑ Mt. 5:42	❑ Mt. 11:29	❑ Mt. 22:39	❑ Lk. 12:20, 21	❑ Jn. 14:1
❑ Mt. 5:46, 47	❑ Mt. 11:30	❑ Mt. 22:40	❑ Lk. 12:32-34	❑ Jn. 14:2
❑ Mt. 5:48	❑ Mt. 12:11, 12	❑ Mt. 23:3	❑ Lk. 12:40	❑ Jn. 14:6
❑ Mt. 6:1	❑ Mt. 12:25	❑ Mt. 23:24	❑ Lk. 13:4, 5	❑ Jn. 14:15
❑ Mt. 6:2	❑ Mt. 12:30	❑ Mt. 23:25, 26	❑ Lk. 14:8	❑ Jn. 14:16, 17
❑ Mt. 6:3, 4	❑ Mt. 12:36	❑ Mt. 23:28	❑ Lk. 14:13, 14	❑ Jn. 14:18
❑ Mt. 6:6	❑ Mt. 12:40	❑ Mt. 23:37	❑ Lk. 14:28	❑ Jn. 14:19
❑ Mt. 6:7, 8	❑ Mt. 13:23	❑ Mt. 24:14	❑ Lk. 15:8	❑ Jn. 14:26
❑ Mt. 6:9	❑ Mt. 13:24, 25	❑ Mt. 24:27	❑ Lk. 15:20	❑ Jn. 14:27
❑ Mt. 6:10	❑ Mt. 13:31, 32	❑ Mt. 24:30, 31	❑ Lk. 16:10, 11	❑ Jn. 15:5
❑ Mt. 6:11	❑ Mt. 13:33	❑ Mt. 24:36	❑ Lk. 16:13	❑ Jn. 15:13
❑ Mt. 6:12	❑ Mt. 13:45, 46	❑ Mt. 25:13	❑ Lk. 16:14, 15	❑ Jn. 16:33
❑ Mt. 6:13	❑ Mt. 13:47	❑ Mt. 25:21	❑ Lk. 16:25	❑ Jn. 17:3
❑ Mt. 6:14, 15	❑ Mt. 13:52	❑ Mt. 25:40	❑ Lk. 17:3	❑ Jn. 20:29
❑ Mt. 6:17	❑ Mt. 13:57	❑ Mt. 26:26-28	❑ Lk. 17:10	❑ Jn. 21:17
❑ Mt. 6:19	❑ Mt. 15:3	❑ Mt. 26:41	❑ Lk. 17:16, 17	❑ Acts 20:35
❑ Mt. 6:20	❑ Mt. 15:5, 6	❑ Mt. 26:53, 54	❑ Lk. 17:26, 27	❑ Rev. 1:8
❑ Mt. 6:21	❑ Mt. 15:11	❑ Mt. 28:19, 20	❑ Lk. 18:7, 8	❑ Rev. 3:20
❑ Mt. 6:25, 26	❑ Mt. 15:14	❑ Mt. 28:20	❑ Lk. 18:14	❑ Rev. 22:20

Patterns and Crafts

These Little Ones (page 125)

Pattern for paper angel cut-out chain:

Cut a piece of 8 ½-by 11-inch paper in half length-wise. Fold accordion-style in four equal sections. Unfold and trace angel pattern on outside fold. Refold and cut out angel (except at the hands). Unfold. You've created an angel chain!

fold
(do not cut)

fold
(do not cut)

The Light of the World (page 224)

Pattern for light switch cover:

Signs to Believers (page 174)
Pattern for doorknob sign:

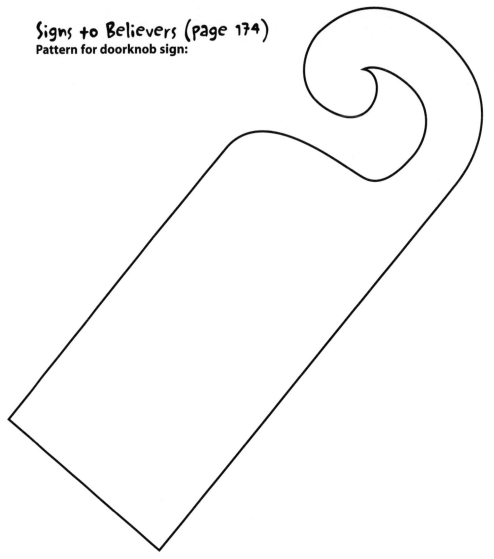

Don't Toot Your Horn (page 50)
Directions for kazoo:
Cover the end of a paper towel tube with wax paper. Wrap a rubber band around the tube to hold the wax paper in place. Poke a hole in the center of the wax paper with a pencil.

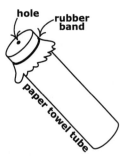

hole
rubber band
paper towel tube

Recipes

Let God Perfect You (page 48)
Bread Dough Clay (Do not eat)

Clay:
6 slices of white bread, crusts removed
6 teaspoons white school glue
$1/2$ teaspoon liquid dishwashing detergent

Coating to prevent cracking:
4 tablespoons glue
1 tablespoon water

Tear the bread into small pieces. Add the glue and dishwashing liquid detergent. Mix together with your hands. If it is too dry, add drops of glue. If it is too sticky, add small pieces from another slice of bread. Mix the coating in a separate bowl. Sculpt the clay into the desired shape and then brush on the coating to prevent cracking.

Take the Plank Out (page 63)
Sawdust Clay

1 cup sawdust
1 cup flour
$3/4$ cup water

Mix ingredients. Shape sculpture. Let sculpture dry for several days. If desired, sand and paint.

Workers for the Harvest (page 81)
Easy Fruit Dip

8 ounces of cream cheese, softened
1 teaspoon vanilla extract
confectioner's sugar
food coloring (optional)

Mix first two ingredients until smooth. Stir in confectioner's sugar until as sweet as desired. Color with a few drops of food coloring. Serve with sliced fruit.

For the Sake of Tradition (page 109)
Command-mints

$\frac{1}{4}$ cup butter or margarine
$\frac{1}{3}$ cup light corn syrup
1 $\frac{1}{2}$ teaspoon peppermint extract
$\frac{1}{2}$ teaspoon salt
4 drops food coloring
5 cups confectioner's sugar

Mix first five ingredients. Stir in the confectioner's sugar. Knead until completely blended. Roll small pieces into balls and flatten on wax paper. Air dry overnight to harden.

Make Disciples (page 159)
Quick Nachos

tortilla chips
1 can refried beans
mild salsa
grated cheese

Preheat oven to 350 degrees. Line cookie sheet with aluminum foil. Spread refried beans on chips. Sprinkle grated cheese. Bake until cheese is melted. Top with salsa and serve!

Easy Popcorn Balls
For memorization celebrations!

3 tablespoons margarine or butter
1 10-oz. bag marshmallows
10 cups popped popcorn
food coloring (optional)

In a large pot, melt the margarine. Add marshmallows and stir until melted. If desired, stir in 2 or 3 drops of food coloring. Remove mixture from heat and stir mixture into a bowl of popped popcorn. Let cool slightly. Butter your hands or spray them with cooking spray. Shape the mixture into popcorn balls. Set the balls on wax paper.

Popcorn balls taste great with homemade root beer, which is easier to make than you might think. You just need root beer extract (from the spice aisle at your grocery store), water, sugar, and dry ice (available in most supermarkets). The recipe is on the extract bottle.

Helping Your Child
Trust Jesus

Explain the following truths to your child. If he understands and believes them, he is probably ready to put his trust in Jesus as his personal Savior and Lord. If so, pray with him. Then call your local church to discuss how your church welcomes children into the family of God. Rejoice! That's what's happening in heaven (Luke 15:10).

1. God loves us and wants us to live forever with him.
"For God so loved the world that he gave his one and only Son, that whoever believes in him shall not perish but have eternal life" (John 3:16).

2. We have sinned.
Anyone, then, who knows the good he ought to do and doesn't do it, sins (James 4:17).

If we claim to be without sin, we deceive ourselves and the truth is not in us (1 John 1:8).

3. Because of our sins, we do not deserve to live forever with God.
For all have sinned and fall short of the glory of God (Romans 3:23).

For the wages of sin is death, but the gift of God is eternal life in Christ Jesus our Lord (Romans 6:23).

4. Jesus died on the cross to take the punishment we deserve. He is the only way to heaven. We can't get there by trying to be good.
He was delivered over to death for our sins and was raised to life for our justification (Romans 4:25).

Jesus answered, "I am the way and the truth and the life. No one comes to the Father expect through me" (John 14:6).

Know that a man is not justified by observing the law, but by faith in Jesus Christ (Galatians 2:16).

Helping Your Child Trust Jesus

5. We need to repent (turn away from sin) and trust Jesus as Savior (the one who saves) and Lord (the one who rules over us).
"I have declared to both Jews and Greeks that they must turn to God in repentance and have faith in our Lord Jesus" (Acts 20:21).

"Salvation is found in no one else, for there is no other name under heaven given to men by which we must be saved" (Acts 4:12).

That if you confess with your mouth, "Jesus is Lord," and believe in your heart that God raised him from the dead, you will be saved (Romans 10:9).

Peter replied, "Repent and be baptized, every one of you, in the name of Jesus Christ for the forgiveness of your sins. And you will receive the gift of the Holy Spirit" (Acts 2:38).

6. If Jesus is our Lord, it will show by how loving we are to others.
This is how we know who the children of God are and who the children of the devil are: Anyone who does not do what is right is not a child of God; nor is anyone who does not love his brother (1 John 3:10).

Whoever does not love does not know God, because God is love (1 John 4:8).

By this all men will know that you are my disciples, if you love one another (John 13:35).

Books by Tracy Harrast

Not-So-Quiet Times: 240 Family Devotions Based on the Words of Jesus
Not-So-Quiet Times: 240 Family Devotions Based on Psalms and Proverbs (available soon)
Picture That! Bible Storybook
My Mommy & Me Story Bible
One to Grow On Series: My Bible ABCs
One to Grow On Series: My Bible Animals
One to Grow On Series: My Bible Colors
One to Grow On Series: My Bible Numbers
Peek-a-Bible: The Lost and Found Lamb
Peek-a-Bible: The Big Boat Ride
Peek-a-Bible: The Christmas Story
Peek-a-Bible: Little David and Big Goliath
Peek-a-Bible: Jonah Goes Overboard
Peek-a-Bible: The Easter Story (available soon)
Peek-a-Bible: Joseph (available soon)
Bible Lessons for Young Readers (with several authors)
Bible Puzzle Time: God's People Become a Nation
The Life and Lessons of Jesus: Jesus Is Born!
The Life and Lessons of Jesus: Jesus Grows Up
The Life and Lessons of Jesus: Jesus Prepares to Serve
The Life and Lessons of Jesus: Following Jesus
The Life and Lessons of Jesus: Name of Jesus
The Life and Lessons of Jesus: Learning to Love Like Jesus
The Life and Lessons of Jesus: Jesus Shows God's Love
The Life and Lessons of Jesus: Jesus Heals
The Life and Lessons of Jesus: Jesus Works Miracles
The Life and Lessons of Jesus: Jesus Teaches Me to Pray
The Life and Lessons of Jesus: Jesus' Last Week
The Life and Lessons of Jesus: Jesus Is Alive!